EAST OF EVEREST

EAST OF EVEREST

An Account of the
New Zealand Alpine Club Himalayan Expedition
to the Barun Valley in 1954

BY

*Sir Edmund Hillary and
George Lowe*

NEW YORK
E. P. DUTTON AND COMPANY, INC.

PRINTED IN ENGLAND

CONTENTS

OVER THE HILLS TO THE BARUN VALLEY

SIR EDMUND HILLARY

TWENTY miles to the east of Everest is the great peak of Makalu, 27,790 ft., and between Everest and Makalu and to the south there is a confused mass of icepeaks and hidden valleys. In 1951 Eric Shipton and I made the first exploration into the fringes of this country. Very early in our trip it became quite clear that the map was completely inaccurate. We found vast glaciers and mountain ranges where nothing was indicated. Enormous valleys drained out through precipitous gorges, but all the map showed were gentle pastures. Obviously the surveyors who produced the map had never been anywhere near the country and had sketched things in with fertile imaginations. But this only increased our enthusiasm to unravel its secrets.

From a camp on the Imja glacier we climbed with some difficulty up on to a high pass and looked for the first time into the great glaciated valley of the Hongu. It looked exciting country. With a light camp we descended steep snow and ice slopes and pitched our tent beside a glacial lake in the floor of the valley. The following day we crossed the Hongu glacier and reached a pass on the far side. It was a remarkable viewpoint. Before us was a tantalising area of peaks, snow plateaux and steep glaciers, all dominated by the wonderful massif of Makalu. We had insufficient resources to go any farther, but we turned back with the determination that some day we would carry on the exploration to the foot of Makalu itself. This small trip was a wonderful experience for me, for not only did I have all the pleasures of exploring new and exciting country, but my companion was Eric Shipton—probably the greatest of modern English explorers and a man whose ability to live and move in mountain country had become a legend in New Zealand as in all the mountaineering world.

Our little trip soon became submerged in more exciting discoveries. We explored the south side of Everest and found a possible route to its summit up the broken icefall of the Khumbu glacier. But my enthusiasm to strike to the east towards Makalu never grew less, and my favourite occupation in quiet moments became the planning of ways and means of achieving it.

In 1952 our opportunity came. The British Cho Oyu expedition was repulsed on its major objective and divided up into smaller parties for climbing and exploration. Eric Shipton, Charles Evans, George Lowe and myself, with a band of Sherpas, crossed again to the Hongu valley and then over our high pass to camp on an extensive snow plateau surrounded by shapely snow peaks and draining down into a deep, gloomy rift under the precipices of Makalu—the Barun valley. From this camp, in two days of sheer pleasure, we climbed three great snow peaks of between 21,000 and 22,000 ft. And from these peaks our eyes seemed always to be drawn inexorably to the giant of the area, one of the loveliest mountains I have seen, a tall, graceful spire of fluted snow and ice. A peak, as George described it, "worthy of an expedition". We called it Baruntse.

We descended into the great ragged trough of the Barun glacier and made a hasty visit to its head. But we did not see much. A heavy fall of monsoon snow blanketed the country and we struggled down to lower levels. We planned to descend the Barun, even though we had no idea of what its lower gorges were like. As we left the glacier behind, we came down into a veritable paradise. For miles we waded through blazing acres of flowering red azaleas. In gaps in the monsoon clouds we caught tantalising glimpses up side valleys, each with its little glaciers and ring of icy peaks. The Barun turned into a great U-shaped trough thickly clothed in pine forests. On both sides innumerable waterfalls hung like slender threads on the sheer rock walls. It was the loveliest valley I had ever seen. In its lower reaches impassable gorges blocked the way and we had to climb out over a 14,000-ft. pass to the west. Here the rhododendrons were still in full bloom and the grassy slopes, freshly clear of snow, were thickly carpeted with primulas of every colour in the rainbow. On this pass the weather cleared for a moment and we were able to look well up into the next valley—the Iswa. Far up we could see many great glaciers and peaks, and we argued fiercely as to how they fitted in with our hazy knowledge of the topography of this unknown region. We left the Barun with the firm conviction that here was the perfect area for climbing and exploration.

George Lowe and I returned to New Zealand and took with us our enthusiasm for the Barun. We were able to impart something of it to the New Zealand Alpine Club, which had for some years been discussing the possibility of sending a Club expedition to the Himalayas. They decided to apply to the Nepalese Government for permission to send an expedition to the Barun valley in 1954 and I was invited to lead it.

The year 1953 was one of some importance to George and me. We were involved in the successful attack on Mount Everest and had little time for planning for the following year. In New Zealand an Expedition Committee had been set up in Dunedin and was quietly but steadily at work building up the foundations for future organisation. When we returned to New Zealand in August 1953 everything was ready for immediate action. We drew up extensive lists of food and equipment; estimates were made of probable sources of finance; and the party itself was chosen. The club's policy was to invite two British climbers and pay all their expenses as a gesture of appreciation of the many generous inclusions of New Zealand climbers in British expeditions. The two men chosen were Dr. Charles Evans, who has an outstanding record in the Himalayas, and Dr. Michael Ball, who was to be the expedition doctor. Charles Evans was invited to be deputy leader of the party. A large number of applications were received from climbers throughout New Zealand, and out of these the main body of the expedition was chosen: Bill Beaven, Geoff Harrow, Norman Hardie, Jim McFarlane, Colin Todd and Brian Wilkins. None of these men had been to the Himalayas before, but all of them had outstanding records on tough exploratory trips and on difficult ice climbs. George Lowe and I brought the number of the party up to ten.

Finance, as always, was the major problem. We estimated the cost would be in excess of £6,000, and in fact it turned out to be nearer £8,000.

All the New Zealand members of the party were asked to contribute £200 each. The rest of the money was made up by lectures, donations, an excellent contract with *The Times* and a very generous donation from the Joint Committee of the Royal Geographical Society and the Alpine Club in London. We were also greatly assisted by many generous gifts of food, clothing and gear.

We were determined to have first-class equipment. We took as our model the Everest Expedition, but modified and improved the equipment to suit our own particular needs. Our tents were the well-tried Meade design, which is rather heavy but very roomy and stable. We had two sizes—the ordinary Meade tent which holds two in comfort, and a larger size which could hold four sahibs or six Sherpas. Our sleeping bags were an improved version of the New Zealand-made model used at 28,000 ft. on Everest, but now using a very light nylon cloth which reduced their weight even more. Our down jackets were made of the same material, and these were a particular success. The Research Association in England which made the Everest high-altitude boots also very kindly continued their development work and produced some extremely satisfactory modifications for us. Although financial considerations barred us from being equipped on a lavish scale, I felt confident that our gear was the best procurable for the tasks we had in mind.

The accumulating and packing of gear both in England and New Zealand was a major task. We were particularly fortunate in having as our secretary in England Bill Packard, a member of Tilman's expedition to Annapurna in 1950. He proved an absolute genius at obtaining favourable terms for us in all our purchases. The majority of the organisation, however, and certainly the burden of worry and responsibility, rested with the committee in Dunedin, and they put in a great deal of work getting together all of the food and clothing, packing it into cardboard cartons, kitbags and wooden boxes, and finally despatching it to the ship. The expedition owed them a great debt of gratitude.

We had two primary objectives. The first was to explore and map as much as possible of the unknown regions around the Barun valley. We knew this would entail tough work in the dense bush and fearsome gorges of the lower valleys—work that could be best carried out by small mobile parties. We intended to carry out a thorough photo-theodolite survey of the areas visited and we hoped to climb as many of the local peaks as we could. Our second objective, to be pursued when the party was well-acclimatised to high altitudes, was to attempt the ascent of one or more of three formidable peaks: Baruntse, 23,570 ft.; Chamlang, 24,012 ft.; and Ama Dablam, 22,310 ft.

Baruntse had a special appeal to us, and to get to grips with it would fulfil the ambition I had had since I first saw the mountain two years before. I knew that its wonderful spire would demand a high standard of icemanship. Chamlang is an enormous mountain—a great, long wall of avalanche-swept precipices. It had never been closely examined, but from a distance it appeared to offer no easy route. One of the valleys we hoped to explore drained the southern slopes of Chamlang, so we planned to search the mountain on this side for a feasible route.

And, finally, we had in mind Ama Dablam. This was unquestionably the most difficult of the lot; its great ice-sheathed rock faces and saw-toothed ridges were familiar and forbidding sights to parties on the way to Everest. Ama Dablam had almost come to be regarded as representing the ultimate in impossibility, but from the Hongu I had noticed what appeared to be a faint breach in its defences and was keen to examine this at shorter range. We felt that success on any one of these peaks would leave us well satisfied.

We all gathered at Jogbani on the Indian-Nepalese border on the evening of 28th March. Most of the party looked very brown and fit after long sea voyages across the Indian Ocean, but Evans, Lowe and I had flown straight from the winter in England and America and looked pale by comparison. Jogbani is at the end of the railway and at this time of the year is particularly hot and dusty. We knew we had to pass through the Indian and Nepalese Customs here, but darkness had fallen and we were unable to find the Customs Officers. As most of our equipment had travelled through India in railway vans sealed by the Customs in Bombay, we did not dare open them without official supervision. It seemed a rather depressing start to the expedition, but we decided we would have to camp the night on the railway platform. At this stage the owner of one of the local jute mills came to our rescue. He offered us the use of his spare bungalow and we accepted with pleasure. Carrying our personal gear, we tramped through the dust for a mile or so and were led to a house which even in the darkness appeared of imposing dimensions. We went inside and found it clean and whitewashed, although sadly lacking in furniture. We were too tired to care. Before long all of us were stretched out on the floor and verandah—not very comfortably perhaps, but feeling quite cheerful and anticipating a good night's sleep.

Our contentment did not last long. From every damp corner and stagnant pool in the town, hoards of huge mosquitoes gathered to feast on our new blood. I am sure I did not sleep for half an hour all night, and by morning we were all an irritable mass of mosquito bites. We were thankful when the light gave us relief from their attacks, and as we consumed a makeshift breakfast our one heartily expressed desire was to get away from the plains as quickly as possible and up into the cool comfort of the hills.

But first we had to complete the official formalities. In this we were helped immensely by the only white man in the district—Mr. Howard Barclay, a young Australian who was running a medical mission with the help of his wife. Mr. Barclay was invaluable. He drove us around over the impossible tracks in his Land-Rover, and in one amazing morning we passed all our gear through the Customs, presented our permit to enter to the Nepalese authorities, drew large sums of money out of the

Bank of Nepal and ordered two large G.M.C. trucks to transport our equipment to the end of the road. I think we must have created a record. To our astonishment the trucks turned up before we expected them—they were only two hours late—and in a last flurry of energy we loaded our four tons of gear on board. Most of the party climbed on to the first lorry and Mr. Barclay's Land-Rover, and to a chorus of shouts and cheers headed off in a cloud of dust towards the hills. A few of us remained to complete the last-minute tasks. Towards evening everything was finished; we clambered aboard the second heavily laden truck and left Jogbani behind.

It is only thirty miles from Jogbani to Dharan—a large bazaar at the foot of the hills—but it is thirty miles of narrow, rutted track, of vast potholes and decaying bridges. Our driver attacked his task with admirable enthusiasm, and sent us lurching and bumping down the road in a fashion that only a very robust vehicle could have withstood. Before long we were covered in a thick layer of dust. We had been travelling for two hours when we drove from daylight into darkness with the suddenness of the tropics. Thatched huts drifted by, dimly lit by small economical fires. Fireflies sparkled amongst the trees and the air was heavy with the scent of the East. Above us the velvet sky was criss-crossed with shooting stars.

Four hours after leaving Jogbani, we bumped up the roughly cobbled main street of Dharan surrounded by a shouting mass of the local inhabitants. The flickering lights, the milling throng and the confusion of voices produced a scene both colourful and chaotic. Our driver exchanged words with some of the gathering and then moved on again through the town and up an even rougher track than before. We reached an open clearing amongst the brush, saw the lights of camp fires and the dim shapes of tents, and soon we were being greeted by some cheerful New Zealand shouts welcoming us to our first camp site. It was a relief to breathe the fresh, dust-free air of the hills. We parted from our truck driver in an atmosphere of mutual dislike . . . he wanted more pay than he had quoted in Jogbani and I did not intend to pay it. I did not ! . . .

We slept out under the stars.

Our two days at Dharan were very busy ones. We were met here by some of our Sherpa porters who had come down from their homes in Darjeeling and in Namche Bazar. It was good to see again our old friend Da Tensing who was to act as sirdar. Many of our Sherpas had been with us on Everest the previous year, and Dawa Thondup, Annullu, Pasang Dawa and Mingma had all carried loads to 26,000 ft.

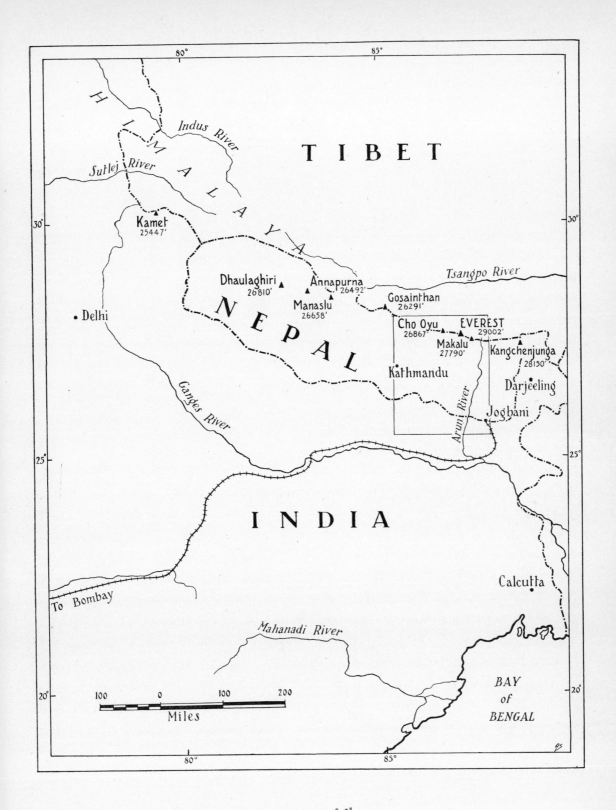

We signed on and equipped fifteen Sherpas for work in the mountains and employed the remaining fifteen as porters for the march in.

Each member of the party had a Sherpa appointed to look after his well-being. This was not regarded with enthusiasm by some of our "sahibs", as most climbers prefer to do everything for themselves. They viewed with some trepidation the thought of having attached to them a Sherpa who would carry their loads, erect their tent, blow up their air-mattresses and even wash their shirts. I overheard McFarlane commenting that he thought his personal man would be rather superfluous. It was surprising how short a time it took for even the most determined individualists to change, and before long their voices were as loud as ours in calling out for a cup of tea or an extra pullover.

Our biggest task at Dharan was the sorting out of all our equipment into loads of sixty to eighty pounds and the hiring of the necessary coolies to carry them. Charles Evans is a competent speaker of Hindustani and he set to work to sign on a hundred coolies. We issued much of the personal gear to the sahibs and Sherpas and the camp rapidly assumed a Christmas air, with everyone admiring their new acquisitions. By the end of the second day, the disorder had at last started to vanish and we were ready to move on.

On the morning of 1st April the camp stirred early into life. Tents were struck, our bedding and personal gear were made up into loads, and breakfast was devoured. As our coolies appeared, they were issued with loads and started off up the valley, and most of the sahibs followed them. The usual unexpected problems arose, and it was not until noon that the last load moved off. Charles Evans and I trailed wearily behind.

The track meandered pleasantly along beside a stream and then shot abruptly up a very long, steep hill. For the first day out after a lecture tour of America I found this a bit tough, and reached the top in a decidedly overheated condition. I was pleased to note that George Lowe was not going noticeably faster than I was. We now dropped steeply down three or four thousand feet into the next valley. Charles Evans and I were travelling together, and quite unconsciously we started going faster and faster. Soon we were leaping and running down, with first one in the lead and then the other. I got to the bottom first—but I bitterly regretted it for the next few days as I dragged my aching muscles around the countryside. Charles seemed much less affected and I secretly conceded him a moral victory.

Our days quickly developed into a comfortable routine. Every morning we were wakened by a cheerful Sherpa thrusting a hot cup of tea into our hands. At 5.30 a.m. the whole party would move briskly off into the cool of the morning and walk steadily for about three hours. The lower hill country of Nepal varies from a rather lush tropical growth, with frequent streams and warm muggy temperatures, to arid stretches of bare clay and stunted trees. But all of it is hot and most of it is steep. The track wound up and down—climbing sharply up the bush-clad hills or descending abruptly down to some turbulent river. In the floors of the valleys and clinging in places to the hillsides were terraced rice and corn fields clustering around a group of thatched houses. But there was little growing now. The dry soil was waiting for the onset of the monsoon in some three months' time.

About 8.30 a.m. we would look around and find a grassy place on which to pitch our canvas awning. There we would rest in comfort while our Sherpa cook produced a substantial breakfast of porridge, fried eggs, biscuits, butter and jam, and tea. We found this a very pleasant time of the day, and always spent two or three hours eating, reading, writing and sleeping. Colin Todd had a great enthusiasm for collecting beetles, and could usually be found vigorously shaking the shrubbery and pouncing on any unfortunate insect that fell off. By 11 a.m. the laden coolies would have caught up to us and gone on ahead, so with considerable reluctance we would emerge into the blazing heat of the noonday sun and set off after them. We found this period of the day made rather uncomfortable travelling, and although we took every opportunity to swim in the cool mountain streams, we arrived at our destination hot, dusty and sticky. We usually chose our camp site beside a stream and had frequent bathes until evening brought us relief from the heat. But life was very pleasant and there was much to interest us as we went along. Our steady marching was hardening up our leg muscles and our shoulders became accustomed to our moderate loads.

A couple of days' travelling brought us to the town of Dhankuta, and then on the morning of 3rd April we reached the crest of a 7,000-ft. pass to find that the haze and cloud had cleared away. Stretching across the horizon from east to west was the great wall of the Himalayas, still white with the winter's snow and looking unutterably cool and remote from our hot dry hillsides. Our excitement was intense. Out came cameras and maps, compasses and binoculars, and great were the arguments as we attempted to identify some of the more prominent peaks. Makalu and Chamlang were easily identified to the east of us, looking particularly impressive. We dropped down off the pass with a renewed enthusiasm to get up into the snows and a distinct feeling of impatience at the slow pace of our coolies.

For several days we followed up the great valley of the Arun river and on 6th April reached the large village of Khanbari, which is perched on a pleasant spur high above the river. Here we planned to change our coolies for a new lot and expected a delay of several days. It is not an easy matter to obtain a large number of coolies at short notice from a relatively sparsely populated countryside, so Evans and I decided to cross the Arun river to the neighbouring village of Dingla and see what we could raise there. We took with us several Sherpas, including our sirdar, Da Tensing. I had been to Dingla three years before with Shipton and at that time the headman had proved friendly and helpful, so we were hopeful that with his assistance we would have no difficulty in recruiting the men we were after.

As we approached the village our Sherpas chatted freely with the local inhabitants, and then informed us that the old headman had gone and that a new one, promoted by Kathmandu for some obscure political reason, reigned now instead. We were led up to his house. After a long wait he made his appearance, surrounded by a group of servile advisers. I have rarely seen a shiftier group of men, and the headman had a weak, cunning face. It was clear from the start that we were not likely to get much help. At first we were advised that there were no men available, but when we persisted in our requests the headman changed his tune and offered to supply them at an exorbitant rate of pay. Charles Evans patiently talked on while I tried to follow their conversation and sadly regretted my lack of skill with the language. It was quite clear that the headman and his advisers were regarding it all as a rather good joke, and one man in particular kept breaking into the conversation with frequent witticisms. After three hours of frustrating discussion the headman agreed to have a hundred men ready for us next morning at the usual rate of pay. But we did not feel very happy, for the chuckles of his advisers followed us out of the compound.

We were back next morning at 10 a.m., but there was no sign of the hundred coolies. After an even longer wait, the headman and his gang made their appearance and renewed their old request for double pay. This was the limit! And then the wit of the party produced his best joke and they all rocked with laughter. It was too much for Charles. His Welsh spirit could stand no more. He leapt up, grabbed the shrinking humorist, kicked him very firmly in the seat of the pants and sent him scuttling off down the path. It was quite apparent now that we could expect no assistance at all in this village, so after a few well-chosen sentences we made our departure.

Our only hope now was to obtain our coolies in Khanbari itself. And here we met with a much happier reception. Men were sent out into the surrounding countryside to spread the news and before long a steady flow of coolies were presenting themselves ready for work. We purchased large supplies of rice, flour, salt and cooking fat. Much of this was unobtainable in the village bazaar, but the farmers' wives from miles around came into our camp carrying their little surplus supplies of grain. And in this fashion we made up all our requirements. We had camped on a grassy flat in the middle of the village and Michael Ball, our doctor, worked solidly from dawn until dusk treating the ailments and ills of the local people. The rest of us sorted out all the loads into a maximum of sixty pounds each, for we wanted the coolies to be able to move reasonably freely in the rough country ahead.

Soon after our arrival we produced one of our most treasured possessions—a rugby football—and started kicking it around the dusty village square. At first the local inhabitants scattered in terror to places of safety inside their houses or up in the branches of trees, but gradually their interest in this strange game grew and we encouraged them to join in. After a rather nervous beginning their enthusiasm flared up and we were practically overwhelmed by a seething mass of them, all fired with the sole ambition of having a hearty kick at the ball. What they lacked in experience and skill was more than replaced by their keenness, and it took a brave man to pick the ball up from the feet of a hundred attacking Nepali forwards. The children in particular developed a great interest in the game and there were few moments in the day when our ears were not being treated to the sound of the punting of a football.

After three days in Khanbari we had obtained all the necessary stores and hired the men to carry them. On 9th April we loaded up one hundred and thirty porters and left the village behind. Our route lay steadily upwards over long, wooded ridges high above the Arun river. The countryside was now much more rugged and the going much more difficult. Sometimes in a break in the heavy clouds we would catch a glimpse of a snowy peak, not so very far away. The valleys we were hoping to explore were only a few days' distance on the other side of the Arun river and we tried to get some general idea of their topography. We were not very successful.

E.E.—2

The weather had become unsettled and the continual heavy clouds and frequent showers of rain did not give us much opportunity for accurate observations. But sometimes early in the morning the weather cleared a little and we gained an impression of a series of rugged valleys, cut by deep gorges and divided from each other by massive rock and icepeaks. It looked exciting and difficult country, and we realised that the exploring and mapping of it was going to be an arduous business.

One night we camped in a damp and desolate spot in the middle of the jungle. We cleared some flat places for our tents and then crawled inside out of the miserable, misty rain. One of the boys noticed some blood seeping through his sand-shoes. He pulled them off and discovered to his horrified gaze our first leeches. There was a hurried search by us all and more fat, distended bloodsuckers were brought to light. I don't think some of the party slept too easily that night.

In order to approach the Barun valley we had first to cross the Arun river. For a day and a half we followed down long, steep spurs for many thousands of feet. When we finally reached the river, the heat and humidity hit us like a blow and drained the energy out of us. The turbulent Arun flowed here between great rock bluffs, and swinging high above the water was a frail-looking bridge made of half a dozen twisted ropes of bamboo. It was a most unstable-looking structure and our confidence in it was not helped by our knowledge of Nepalese ideas of maintenance. Their idea is that any bridge is satisfactory until it falls in. We could see the remnants of a previous bridge lying on the river bed far below and wondered if any unfortunate passenger had been carried down with it. Da Tensing and I examined the bridge carefully. It seemed to be in a rather dilapidated condition, so we crossed it to examine it more closely. Holding on to two of the ropes and walking on a third, we shuffled along feeling decidedly insecure and very conscious of the rushing waters below. In several places the bridge was badly in need of repair and we knew that our coolies would have great difficulty in crossing. We were met on the far side by a group of local inhabitants, and after an animated discussion Da Tensing informed me that they were prepared to mend the bridge for quite a modest sum. I accepted their offer with relief, and the men disappeared off into the jungle to return with bundles of bamboo and long creepers. When the bridge was ready we started persuading our coolies to cross. They were understandably reluctant to do so. Sweeping showers of rain were making the bridge slippery and treacherous, and the men wanted to be paid off. After five hours of shouting and cajoling we got them all over,

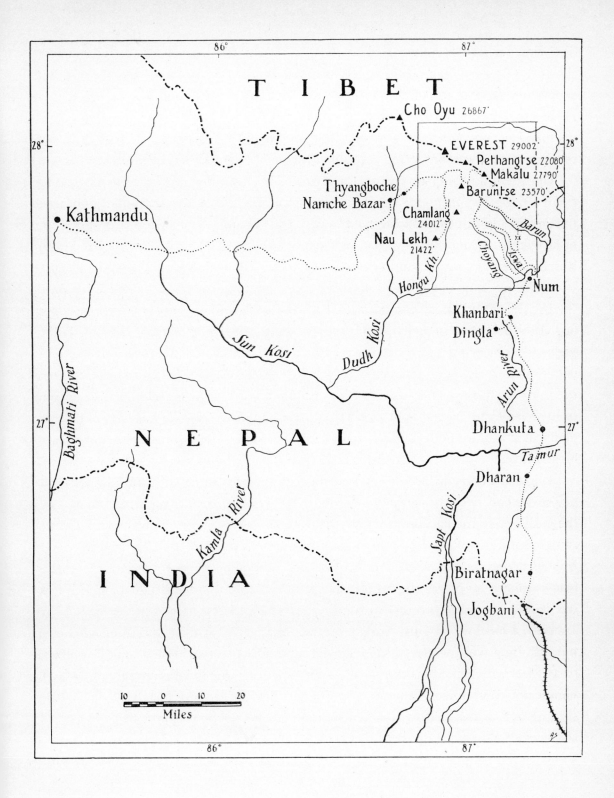

and with a great feeling of relief climbed up to our next camp site a thousand feet above the river. Two days later we reached the village of Sedua, five thousand feet above the Arun. From here on, our path was to lie continuously upwards into the snow and our real work would begin.

Many of our coolies were now rather tired and losing heart. The sight of heavy snow on the hilltops not so far above us obviously frightened them a good deal and we had great difficulty in persuading them to go on. Some, in fact, refused to do so and we had to pay them off. The situation was looking rather critical and it appeared that we wouldn't get any loads past Sedua. Da Tensing now rose to the occasion. In a fine burst of oratory he calmed the nervous coolies and persuaded some of the local people to fill in the gaps in our porters' ranks. The day was saved!

At Sedua the first of our exploratory parties was to break off from the main group. Charles Evans and Geoff Harrow were taking six Sherpas and three weeks' supplies of food and striking to the west into the Choyang valley. Our glimpses of this valley had made it clear that they might experience considerable difficulty in getting into it, but they were a strong, mobile and well-equipped party. After they had explored the Choyang valley we hoped they would find a way on to the Hongu glacier and from there examine the approaches to Chamlang and Ama Dablam. Their trip, as planned, was a long and arduous one, but it would help us to fill in a very large blank on the map.

The main body of porters and stores was to cross into the Barun valley by a 14,000-ft. pass over the ridge between the Iswa and the Barun. This approach evaded the great gorges the Barun river had cut out in its lower reaches, and was actually the route George Lowe and I had used with Eric Shipton in 1952. But now the pass was heavily covered with winter snow and looked a much more formidable problem. From Sedua a long, bumpy, wooded ridge ran steeply up towards the pass, and this we intended to follow.

On the morning of 14th April I was up very early, stirring the camp into life, but progress was painfully slow. Evans and Harrow, with their small, efficient party, were soon ready and we farewelled them with envious comments as we viewed our own huge piles of baggage and the disorganised bunch of chattering coolies. As quickly as possible we started our loads moving and little groups of coolies disappeared off up the track. Da Tensing was magnificent. Some of the coolies disappeared during the night and a few loads remained, but he managed to recruit a few more men in the village and finally achieved his greatest triumph when he persuaded the headman himself to carry the last load. The morning was fine and warm, and we climbed slowly upwards along pleasant forest tracks lined with crimson rhododendrons and great waxy magnolias. Under foot the turf was vivid with primulas and gentians. But the weather was too good to last and before long it was raining again. The track became slippery and muddy, and the mist blanketed out the view. Despite the rain, we were a little concerned about water for our next camp. All the streams in the bush seemed to be dry, and a hundred men require a lot of water.

Wilkins and I went on ahead and suddenly came upon a little grassy clearing. It looked an ideal camp site, but we still hadn't found any water. As we were looking around, a magnificent grazing yak snorted at us and then tossed its head and walked off into the bush. We found a small pool and decided it would have to do. A heavy shower was approaching, so we quickly spread out some large canvas covers and before long we had a good pool on each of them. We drained this water off into some containers, and although it had a slightly oily flavour we thought it a good deal safer than the muddy hole we had found. Our camp was at about 9,000 ft. and the crest of the ridge was still about 1,500 ft. above us. In the later afternoon we climbed up the steep slopes and looked over the narrow crest. On the far side, shrouded in mist, was the Iswa valley—obviously narrow and precipitous. We intended exploring it, but it looked a tough problem.

The rain cleared the air of haze, and next morning was sharp and invigorating. It was an excellent opportunity really to see something. Carrying one of our photo-theodolites, we climbed quickly up on to the ridge and then started along it. We were now crossing frequent snowdrifts and having to kick steps up the steeper slopes. We could see a few clouds gathering, and this spurred us on to greater speed. Panting with our efforts, we raced up on to a great bump at 11,700 ft.

The view was worth all the effort. From here we first saw the upper Iswa valley, and it was a dramatic and sobering sight. Beneath us, the Iswa river poured through a narrow gorge heavily clothed in bush. Higher up, the gorge widened a little into a U-shaped valley, with forested floor and terrific rock walls. But inevitably our attention was drawn to the gleaming white peaks at the head of the valley—the sharp, icy spire of Peak 6 and the enormous glaciated south face of Chamlang. The glaciers at the head of this valley were almost completely out of sight around a sharp corner and there was still much of the valley's topography that we could not understand. The Iswa party was going to have an interesting time.

The ridge now descended steeply for about 700 ft. and, being out of the sun, was deeply covered in snow. I knew our barefooted coolies would be reluctant to descend it, but there was no suitable place to camp on the bump. I decided to push on with the Sherpas and hope that the coolies would follow. It was a risk, but it succeeded. We established our camp on a little saddle at about 11,000 ft., and the coolies, none the worse for their brief trip over the snow, carried all the loads down to us. Bad weather was approaching and we decided to pay them off as quickly as possible so that they could get back to more comfortable levels. We set up a few boxes as a table, got out our book of names and untied some money bags. But we were too late. There was a clap of thunder and next moment we were being pelted with torrential hail. The poor coolies, in their light garments, were looking thoroughly miserable and we knew they couldn't stand too much of this cold weather. We hastily put up a few umbrellas and went on paying out their money. As each man received his dues, plus a generous *baksheesh*, he touched his forehead in thanks and farewell, and then dashed off in a flurry of bare legs up the long snow slope and then down into the protection of the bush.

I had asked George Lowe to take a party made up of Hardie, Beaven and Todd into the Iswa valley. They immediately set to work to organise their trip. Food and equipment were sorted out and made up into sixty-pound loads. It made quite a pile. as they planned to be away for two and a half weeks. They decided that they would need six Sherpas and six coolies to carry it all. Early next morning they loaded up and dropped steeply down from our saddle towards the Iswa gorge through thick forest carpeted with heavy snow.

There were now only four sahibs left—Ball, McFarlane, Wilkins and myself— and our main job was to get all our gear over into the Barun and up to a Base Camp. Our biggest problem was the shortage of porters. We still had some twenty-two Sherpas with us and we'd managed to persuade fourteen of the men from Sedua to remain with us. They did not have any boots, but after a lot of fossicking around we managed to equip most of them with socks and sandshoes. In order to move all our equipment with thirty-six porters, we were going to have to make four relays. I decided that Wilkins and I could handle this part of the carry, and suggested to

McFarlane and Ball that they take a light camp and go on ahead into the Barun and do some mapping.

At 8.15 a.m. I left with the first relay. The ridge rose in two great humps, both well covered in snow. In several long, steep gullies the snow was very firm, and I cut long lines of steps. It was hard work for the men, but they seemed in good spirits. After three hours I reached the top of the second hump. Ahead of me was a long, narrow ridge covered in snow and blocked by a number of rock towers. When the porters arrived they expressed their dislike of the way ahead in no uncertain terms and wanted to go back. I explained that I would make a safe route for them and finally, after a good deal of talking, thirty-five men came along with me and four returned. I started chipping a line of steps along the ridge. In places I had to cut down on to the face in order to get around the rock towers, but the men had now entered into the spirit of the thing and followed along without difficulty. At 1.15 p.m. we had reached about 13,000 ft. and I decided to make the dump on a stretch of the ridge which was clear of snow. There was short scrub here which could be used as firewood and this would save our kerosene. McFarlane and Ball pitched a tent, and with Sherpa Angje settled in for a few days' camping. I returned with the porters to the saddle camp.

That evening, at 5 p.m., we had our first intercamp radio communication. McFarlane from the dump up on the ridge came in loud and clear on my powerful little portable radio. He had nothing to report except that the weather was fine, that they were quite comfortable and the view was breath-taking. And then to our pleasure George Lowe's vigorous voice broke in from the depths of the Iswa. He reported that they had experienced difficult going in dense bush and amongst steep bluffs. After a lot of work they had found a way down through the cliffs to the river. They were now reasonably comfortably camped and intended to push up the river in the morning.

On 17th and 18th April Wilkins and I and our party carried more loads up the ridge, although the weather was rather wet and boisterous. We made such good progress that on the 19th we evacuated the saddle camp and moved the remainder of our gear up to the 13,000-ft. dump. It was quite difficult making sufficient accommodation on the ridge for over forty men, but we finally succeeded in getting them all under some sort of cover, whether it was a tent, awning or a rough shelter constructed from a few cases of food. In the evening the mist cleared and a glorious view unfolded. We were far above a tumbled layer of cloud which stretched unbroken to the east. And on the horizon loomed the huge bulk of Kangchenjunga, glowing pink in the setting rays of the sun. It seemed too beautiful to be real and I stayed there watching it until the cold drove me into the comfort of my sleeping bag. I was unable to contact George on the radio and guessed his party must have turned the corner in the Iswa valley and be approaching the glaciers.

McFarlane and Ball had had an interesting and useful time. For the purpose of mapping the area they had climbed two easy peaks up near the Barun pass, one of 15,000 ft. and one of 16,000 ft. They did extensive surveying with the photo-theodolite from both these summits. When they were coming down from the first peak they saw an animal moving across the slopes below them. It was only about a hundred feet away and they realised that it was a snow leopard. This beautiful animal is rarely seen, so they watched with interest as it padded easily across the steep snow. They estimated that it was about the same size as a large dog, such as an Alsatian. Perhaps a little to their relief, it took no interest in them and disappeared off into the head of the valley.

Our next big task was to get our thirty-eight porters over the pass into the Barun. This had all the appearance of being a tough problem, as a steep and extensive snow-field lay between us and the pass. I was rather unhappy at the thought of having our lightly-clothed men caught in a blizzard in these exposed regions, but the men themselves seemed quite keen to go on. I decided that the least I could do was to pay off the six men who had carried loads this far without any sort of footgear. Their reaction was one of scorn. They assured me that they thought nothing of travelling on the snow in bare feet and asked that they be permitted to continue with the party. Their confidence was infectious, and as their help would be invaluable I acquiesced. But I resolved that we would not set out unless the weather looked calm and settled.

The night was unusually cold, and when I put my head out of the tent in the early morning the sky was clear and there was a hard frost. To the east a faint glow warned us of the sun. It looked as though the weather was being kind to us. I stirred the camp into activity, and after a quick breakfast Wilkins and I sorted out loads and issued them to the porters. By the time the sun had reached us we were almost ready to go. We gave each man some snowglasses and a pair of gloves. The snow slopes ahead were gleaming and hard under the frost and I knew a slip by one of our porters would take a lot of stopping. So I commenced cutting a veritable staircase. Wilkins undertook a roving commission and watched the porters over the difficult stretches. But his help was rarely needed. The porters walked along the steps cheerfully and confidently, and confirmed our belief that these Sedua men were unusually strong and hardy.

After we had been going for an hour the sun had become quite hot and the slope had softened a little. But there was still a thousand feet of steep snow slopes to climb. I went on cutting long zigzags. In places the snow had melted and there were short pitches of easy rock which gave us some pleasant scrambling, but most of the time we were on the snow. After two hours' travelling from camp we reached the crest of the saddle. Well below us was a large snow-covered lake and beyond it the slopes climbed up again to the Barun pass. We rested in the warm sun and I noticed that our barefooted men seemed quite indifferent to the snow on their feet. The clouds were starting to form again, but we had a wonderful view up the Iswa of Chamlang and Peak 6, and I wondered what George and the boys were finding up there.

An hour later we were on the pass itself and looking abruptly down into the Barun valley. Wilkins and I glissaded merrily down long, easy snow slopes, and the porters, thankful to be on the downward grade, plunged and slid down behind us, raising the echoes with cheerful shouts. Soon we were down into the trees again and slithering along snowy aisles shaded by the crimson heads of the rhododendrons. We could hear the roar of the river now and started descending the long, steep gullies of hard, packed snow which dropped sharply down towards it. It was clear that a slip on one of these gullies could prove decidedly dangerous, so with a thought to our illshod coolies we kicked a safe line of steps down the snow. We were all tired when we camped late in the evening on a terrace beside the river, but it was good to lie on the soft grass again and be lulled off to sleep by the soothing roar of the water.

We walked up the Barun valley next morning and I was elated to find it was just as beautiful as I had remembered it. High above us on both sides were tremendous rock precipices and jagged ice ridges. But the valley was green and the air was fresh with the scent of pine trees. For two days we climbed steadily upwards beside the tumbling river. The trees gave way to shrubs and mossy turf cut by wide shingle fans and turbulent glacier streams. Finally we picked our Base Camp at a height of about 15,500 ft. and pitched our tents on a mossy ledge beside the river. It was certainly one of the most dramatic camp sites I have ever used, for towering 12,000 ft. about our heads was Makalu with its fantastic rock ridges and iceclad face.

We were not the only party in the Barun. Four hundred yards upstream, on a wide, grassy ledge, was the Base Camp of the Californian Himalayan Expedition. This expedition had as its objective the ascent of Makalu, and from our camp we could see them like tiny dots on the lower glaciers of the mountain as they established their camps and built up supplies for an attack on the south ridge. We exchanged visits with them and found them a cheerful good-natured party. They gave us a lurid account of their trip into the valley. In order to escape the problem of taking poorly equipped coolies over high snow passes, as we had done, they entered the valley lower down and had a harrowing time in a series of fearsome gorges. They told us that the only reason they had managed to get through was that for long stretches the river was bridged by great quantities of avalanche snow and they walked along this. We watched their progress on the mountain with considerable interest. The south ridge looked exceptionally difficult and we were not really surprised when, after a gallant attempt, they were forced to abandon their efforts after reaching a height of about 23,000 ft.

A CHAPTER OF ACCIDENTS

SIR EDMUND HILLARY

Now that our Base Camp was established, I was able to hand over to Da Tensing, our sirdar, the task of conducting the porters back again to the dump on the ridge for more loads. Meanwhile Wilkins, McFarlane and I with five Sherpas set off up the Barun glacier on a reconnaissance. At this stage we were not by any means accustomed to altitude and our miseries were aggravated by the fact that we were carrying loads of forty pounds or more. The first day we did not get very far and were very happy to camp when we did on a cramped stretch of shingle amongst the boulders on the glacier. Next day our progress was not much better, and as I looked at the agonising efforts of my two companions who had not experienced the delights of altitude before, I could not help wondering if they were thinking with nostalgia of the hills of home. We camped on a terrace on the east side of the Barun at nearly 18,000 ft. We were thoroughly tired of our loads and decided to have a day off them and do a climb instead. There was an interesting peak right behind our camp.

We started off next morning up the ridge directly above us. For the first 1,500 ft. we had easy scrambling over loose boulders, but the altitude made it seem hard work and the pace was very slow. Then the angle abruptly steepened and we put on the rope. Dawa Thondup was with us and I asked him if he would like to come up any farther just for the climb. He took one look up ahead and said he would go if he had to but otherwise he would prefer to wait until we returned. We left him making himself very comfortable in a sunny little cleft in the rocks. The three of us went on and were soon at grips with a rock and ice ridge that seemed all too formidable to us in our unacclimatised condition. But we hacked a way up it and finally dragged ourselves to the summit—20,370 ft. The view made all our efforts almost seem worth while. To the north-west were Everest and Lhotse, well covered with snow and with long, trailing plumes of cloud from their summits. But perhaps of more immediate interest was our view of the enormous west face of Makalu, and we were able to solve many of the problems that had puzzled us. One thing at least was clear—the small Makalu glacier below us gave quite an easy way of approach towards the north ridge of the mountain, although the access on to the ridge itself, from our position anyway, looked decidedly formidable. We descended cautiously down the long summit ridge to Dawa Thondup, and then unroped and with a surge of energy jumped from boulder to boulder back to camp.

Next day we moved farther up the Barun glacier and camped near its head at a height of about 18,800 ft. From this camp McFarlane, Wilkins and I set off to climb an obviously easy peak to the north-east which we felt would give us an excellent idea of the whole of the Barun néve. It proved to be more of a mound of rubble than a peak, and after a long, dull slog up shingle slopes and an easy snow ridge we reached the top—20,300 ft. It was a very valuable viewpoint and Jim McFarlane regretted the fact that he had not brought his photo-theodolite along. To the north-east were several easily accessible passes and McFarlane was eager to have a look over one of them into Tibet. His enthusiasm was infectious and Wilkins agreed to accompany him. I wanted to return to camp and get things organised, for we were planning to commence our return trip down the valley the same afternoon. They roped up and headed off towards the pass, and with a final word that they should not be too late I plunged off down the easy side of the mountain and back to camp.

The afternoon passed very slowly. At 4 p.m. I crawled out of the tent and searched the glacier for signs of Wilkins and McFarlane, but I could not see anything. I felt a surge of anger. What could they be doing? I had told them to get back early and now the afternoon was nearly gone. We could not possibly go down the valley to-day. Feeling somewhat disgruntled, I crawled back into the tent. Time passed and there was no sign of them. My anger had changed to worry. The clouds were down around the peaks and the weather was dull and gloomy. I decided to set a deadline. If they had not turned up by six o'clock I would go and look for them. It was getting cold now and I crawled inside my sleeping bag and was soon snug and warm. At 5.30 p.m. I heard a faint shout. It was one of the boys! I wriggled out of my bag and struggled through the door of the tent. Staggering into camp was Wilkins. He was alone. With a tight feeling in the pit of my stomach, I saw that his face was covered with blood.

"Where's Jim?"

"We fell down a crevasse. I got out, but Jim is still down there."

We got Wilkins into the tent and gave him a drink, and he told me the story.

After they left me they had crossed over the head of the glacier and up on to a little saddle on the main divide. From there, much to their excitement, they had been able to look far out on to the high plateau and peaks of Tibet. After enjoying the view to the full they had turned to come home. They were tired and suffering a little from the effects of altitude, but the glacier seemed to have no crevasses and they plugged dully downwards thinking of nothing but reaching the camp and resting. Wilkins was leading, with only a short stretch of rope, thirty or forty feet, separating him from McFarlane. They were reaching a crest on the glacier where it dropped off rather more steeply, when suddenly without warning Wilkins stepped on a thin crust of snow which concealed a great crevasse. He had no memory of falling, but found himself squatting in deep, loose snow sixty feet down at the narrow bottom of the crevasse. Beside him was McFarlane. Wilkins examined himself and found that despite his terrific fall he seemed comparatively unhurt, although his snowglasses had cut his forehead and he was having trouble in keeping the blood out of his eyes. He examined McFarlane and found that he was having some difficulty in moving at all. It was obvious that he was either badly bruised or had broken something.

Wilkins set to work to try to make a way out. It was quite impossible to get out of the hole down which they had fallen. The crevasse in places was very wide and narrowed at the top with overhanging lips of ice. He started working his way along the crevasse to where it narrowed. Wriggling through small ice passages and scrambling along a snowy ledge which clung to the wall of the crevasse, he made considerable height. Above him the sky was cut off by a thin roof of snow. On every side great unstable-looking masses of snow and ice hung menacingly. It was a horrifying place, but he had to get out. Cutting steps in the walls of the crevasse he inched his way upwards, fearful that at any moment he might dislodge an avalanche that would sweep him to the bottom again. He was aiming for a point where there was a hole in the roof. After two hours of difficult and nerve-racking work he reached the hole and started dragging himself out. At the last moment he felt the snow giving way under him and frantically clawed his way to the surface, leaving his ice-axe sunk in the snow behind. He could do nothing for McFarlane, who was too injured to help himself. The only thing to do was to get help. Lying up on the edge of the crevasse was McFarlane's ice-axe, so Wilkins picked it up and then carefully and cautiously made his way across to the edge of the glacier. Tired and shocked as he was, his trip down the rough boulders beside the glacier must have been a nightmare. The climb up to the tents took the last of his strength.

I looked anxiously at the sky. The weather was still dull and night was not far off. I felt a great sense of urgency. We must get up and find the hole in the glacier before darkness fell. I shouted instructions at our five Sherpas and then quickly bundled together two sleeping bags, some ropes, food and water. I made sure the Sherpas had all their warm clothing, for I knew we could not be back until long after dark. We dropped down from the camp and started off up the rocks beside the glacier. The loose, rolling boulders made for tiring and exasperating travelling. To my worried mind they seemed to be deliberately hindering our progress. The light was already getting very dim and I raced on ahead of the Sherpas, impelled by the fear that we might not find the crevasse. I was searching anxiously now for some sign of tracks, and suddenly to my relief I saw Wilkins's hat on top of a boulder and a set of uneven tracks leading off into the dim whiteness of the glacier. I stifled my urge to follow them and waited impatiently for the Sherpas to catch up. We put on the rope and then I cautiously started along Wilkins's steps. They led far out across the glacier. The light now was very bad. It was almost dark and I berated myself for having arrived too late. "Now we will never find him!" And then I noticed, fifty feet in front of us, a small, round, black hole in the snow. "It must be the one!" I rushed over towards it, but the Sherpas were holding me firmly with a tight rope. Wilkins had warned me about the overhanging lips of the crevasse, so I lay down on my stomach and wriggled slowly over to the hole. I looked down into a black void.

"Hello, Jim!"

For one awful moment there was no reply and then, to my intense relief, a faint voice came from far below. I asked him how he was. His replies were strangely hesitant but seemed quite rational. He said he was quite comfortable, that he was not badly hurt at all, but he thought he had a broken finger. His main trouble was that he was feeling rather thirsty. I pulled my torch out of my pocket and shone it down-wards. The cold, gleaming walls of the crevasse sprang into life, and with a shock I realised how deep it was. I could not see the bottom. McFarlane called up that he could see the light or the reflection of it. I told him I would lower a rope down. I crawled back to the Sherpas, got another rope and then returned to the hole. I was not very happy about my position, because with the torch I could see that I was lying on top of a thin corniced lip. If that broke off it would probably engulf

McFarlane. I lowered the rope carefully down the crevasse. It disappeared out of the range of my light but still went on down. McFarlane did not seem to be able to get it. His voice sounded very weak now and at times rather aimless. I tried swinging the rope around desperately in the hope that it would strike him and he could get hold of it, but with no result.

I crept back from the hole and thought what to do. It was pitch-dark now. The wind was whistling over the glacier and it was bitterly cold. The Sherpas, despite all their clothes, were obviously unhappy and miserable. Their morale did not seem too high. I decided the only thing to do was to go down the crevasse myself. I explained this to them in detail in my faltering Hindustani. They would lower me on two ropes. When I reached the bottom I would tie McFarlane on one of the ropes and they were to pull him to the surface. Then they could pull me up. They obviously understood my instructions, but tried to persuade me against going down. I ignored their pleas.

I tied the two ropes around me and wriggled once again over to the hole in the ice, and then, with a hollow feeling of insecurity, I pushed myself over the edge and dropped into the hole. The ropes came tight and I hung free, unable to reach either wall of the crevasse. I immediately realised I had made a mistake. I had tied the ropes around my waist instead of taking most of the weight around my thighs or feet. Already the rope was cutting into me, crushing my chest and restricting my breathing, but I thought I could stick it out long enough to get down to the bottom of the crevasse. I yelled to the Sherpas to lower me, and slowly, in a series of great jerks, I dropped down. I seemed to go on for ever. The crevasse had narrowed now and I could touch one of the smooth hard walls. And then the Sherpas stopped lowering and I just hung there, gasping like a fish. With all my strength I yelled at them to lower me farther, but they would not move. I twisted frantically on the end of the rope to ease the strain. I knew I could not last for long and I started thinking, "What a funny way to die". The Sherpas still ignored my shouts to lower me farther so I called out for them to pull me up. At first there was no response. Then from below me McFarlane's voice joined in shouting "*Uppa uppa*", and like an answer to a prayer I started moving upwards. I must have transmitted something of my urgency to the Sherpas, for they were pulling with all their strength and I gained height rapidly. Then I jammed under the overhanging lip of the crevasse. The rope was cutting into the edge and held me immovably. The Sherpas panicked once again.

Tugging like madmen, they tried to wrench me free. Something had to give, and I could feel my ribs bending under the fierce pressure of the rope and a sharp pain in my side. I yelled to them once again to ease off a little, and after some long moments they obeyed. The smooth, slippery ice gave no purchase to my flaying hands, but with a tremendous wriggle I managed to get an arm over the top of the crevasse and my eyes rose above the edge. In the blackness I could see dimly the straining figures of the Sherpas, but I could not move any farther. Still suspended from the rope, I could feel all my strength draining out of me. With an impassioned plea that would have done credit to Romeo and Juliet, I tried to persuade one of the Sherpas to come over closer so that I could grasp him with my hand, but they all refused to move nearer the edge. I started wriggling again and somehow got my other elbow above the surface. And then they pulled me out like a cork from a bottle. I have had few better moments than that—lying exhausted on the ice at 19,500 ft., feeling the air flood into my released lungs, with the chattering Sherpas pouring water down my throat.

It was not long before some of my strength came back and I started racking my brains to decide what next to do. The Sherpas were tired and cold, and their morale could not be relied on. It seemed as if our chances of getting McFarlane out were very slim ones. I slid over to the hole once again and shouted down to McFarlane:

"We may have to leave you down there for the night, Jim. If we lower down a couple of sleeping bags, do you think you will be all right?"

There was the usual long pause and then Jim's weak but cheerful reply that he would be quite comfortable. I tied the rope around two sleeping bags and started lowering them carefully over the edge. They seemed to go on for ever and soon disappeared out of the range of my torch. The rope came slack and I knew that they had reached the bottom. McFarlane called out that he had managed to get hold of them and that he had got the rope too. Why not pull him out then? I called down and asked him to tie the rope around his waist. I knew it was taking a risk because he might not be capable of tying it properly, but it was worth a try. It was many minutes before McFarlane's voice told me he thought he was safely tied on. I signalled to the Sherpas to start pulling in the rope.

They took in the slack and next moment McFarlane was on his way up. With growing excitement I grabbed hold of the rope and added my weight to the Sherpas! And then the rope stopped. McFarlane must be jammed under the overhanging

edge. I crawled to the edge and peered over. The rope was cutting in deeply and I
could not see anything. I tried jerking to free it, but to no avail, and then out of the
darkness appeared McFarlane's questing hand. Stretching down, I just managed to
touch it before it fell listlessly away again and some dreadful choking sounds came
from under the ice. We must lower him down again! I shouted desperately at the
Sherpas and, startled into life, they commenced lowering with a rush. In a minute
the rope came slack and McFarlane was on the bottom again.

I crawled over to the edge and shouted down. It was a long time before he replied. His voice was weak, but seemed somehow indestructible and cheerful. He said
he had had a few bad moments up top, but that now he was all right. He would
have to spend the night down there. I told him to crawl into the sleeping bags and
he said that he would. I waited a few moments and then asked him if he was getting
into them; there was a pause and he said "Yes". We anchored the end of McFarlane's rope solidly into the ice and then started slowly downwards. I felt bruised
and weak and it was painful to breathe, but worse than this was the awful sense of
shame in having to leave poor McFarlane sixty feet down in the ice. My only con-
solation was the two sleeping bags which should keep him safe and warm.

The trip back to the tents was a nightmare. The Sherpas were almost as tired
as I was, and we slid and fell over the loose rocks. It took us a long time to get up to
the tents. I crawled in beside Wilkins and got into the comfort and security of my
sleeping bag. The thought of McFarlane dominated my mind and I felt sure I would
never sleep. But Nature was kind and my head had barely touched my rough pillow
before I had fallen into a deep sleep.

I woke with a start and looked at my watch. It was still dark and the wind was
flapping vigorously at the tent. It was about 4.30 a.m. I undid the zip and looked out
—there was a swirling mist of light snow. My chest felt stiff and painful, but I
knew we must get moving, for a heavy fall of snow could prove disastrous. I wakened the Sherpas and we started a cooker going. Wilkins was much refreshed. In
the dim morning light we left the tent and started off into the driving snow. I was
relieved to find it was fairly light, and did not think it would trouble us much. We
were all travelling slowly and it was a long and bitter grind over the loose rocks,
but as we went, it cleared, and when we reached the side of the glacier we could
actually see the little black hole several hundred yards out.

Wilkins and I roped together. I think both of us had the same thought, but neither of us had uttered it. Would McFarlane still be alive? Wilkins carefully belayed me and I wriggled once again on my stomach over to the edge of the hole and looked down. In the morning light I could see the smooth hard shining walls of ice dropping down, but at the bottom it was still dark. I shouted a greeting. There was a long pause and then, to my intense relief, a faint reply—thank God, he was still alive! And then to my amazement McFarlane called out that he had had quite a good night, but he was feeling a little cold now and rather thirsty. "It won't take us long to get you out, Jim."

I conferred with Wilkins. We were still very much afraid of dislodging the corniced edge of the crevasse and engulfing McFarlane. Wilkins, with great courage, offered to descend by the very dangerous route by which he had made his escape and to try and get McFarlane through that way. On one end of the rope we made a sling to put under his thighs to take his weight and then, after arranging a code of signals, we watched him climb cautiously into the second jagged hole fifty feet to the right. He slowly disappeared from view. For an eternity we seemed to let the rope out, and well over a hundred feet had gone before he signalled that he had reached McFarlane. It was a long time before the signal came to pull in the rope, and we tugged and hauled with all our strength. But all that came to the surface was Wilkins himself. He had a depressing story to tell. He had managed to reach McFarlane, but only after great difficulty. The route was quite impossible for anyone not possessed of his full strength and agility. McFarlane was unable to help himself. Contrary to what he had told me, he had not got into his sleeping bags but had just draped them over his knees. He had taken his gloves off his hands and they were cold and stiff. It gave him a good deal of pain in the back to be moved and he was obviously suffering from concussion. This was bad news. Wilkins had tied a sling around McFarlane and he considered the only chance was to lower a rope straight down the other hole and hope that McFarlane could clip it on to the sling.

We moved to the other hole again and lowered the rope. McFarlane got it and called out that he had attached it. We started pulling him in. We were all much fresher and stronger now and the rope came in rapidly, and then it jammed. McFarlane was stuck under the overhang. Wilkins leaned alarmingly over the edge and tried frantically to release it, but it was useless, and we lowered McFarlane right down to the bottom again. We would just have to take the risk of cutting some of the edge away! Carefully held on two ropes, Wilkins and Da Thondup chipped away the edge, trying to make the falling pieces of ice as small as possible. They cut it back about a foot without anything major falling off, so we decided to give it another go. Up McFarlane came. He reached the cornice and jammed once more. I leaned over the edge. There he was, only a short distance below me. Leaning hard out on the rope, I stretched down and managed to get a hand on the slings around his body. Exerting all my strength I pulled him outwards. He came loose and the next moment with a mighty tug he was pulled out over the edge.

We carried him over to a bed we had made. His clothing was frozen and hard, so we dressed him in warm clothing of our own. His hands and feet were the greatest worry. His hands, which had been battered by the fall down the crevasse, were whitish-blue and frozen stiff like claws. When we removed his boots his feet were hard and lifeless, but in spirit he was as strong and cheerful as ever and he jokingly commented that he much preferred being carried down the glacier to walking. We knew we must get him down as quickly as possible—down into the denser air of lower altitudes and back to the ministrations of Dr. Michael Ball. We tied three pack frames together with a rope into a rough stretcher. On this we placed an inflated air-mattress. Jim was by now inside a sleeping bag and we gently lifted him on to the stretcher.

We dragged him over the glacier to the edge of the rocks and started carrying him down. It was terribly hard work. Carrying a man at any time is a difficult business, but at over 19,000 ft. it was most exhausting. The five Sherpas worked magnificently, and Wilkins and I took turns as a sixth man on the stretcher. We rarely made more than fifty feet, slipping and crashing over the boulders, before we would have to have a rest and stop, gasping for breath. My chest was hurting me abominably and Wilkins seemed at the end of his tether. It was obvious that we could never reach our camp, so when we finally gained a flat stretch of gravel with a small stream running through it we left McFarlane there with Wilkins to look after him and the Sherpas and I crossed over and climbed slowly up to our tents. The first necessity was to get medical aid.

Four of the Sherpas set to work packing up all the tents to move the camp back to McFarlane. The remaining Sherpa, Kancha, and I had a quick meal and then, carrying light packs, started off down the valley. Spurred on by my apprehension, I set a fast pace down the terraces above the Barun glacier. It was snowing again and there was a strong and bitter wind, but the going was fairly easy. Then we dropped down on to the moraine of the glacier and had to jump from boulder to shifting boulder. With every jump my chest seemed to burst with pain, and I started dropping behind. I knew I could not get down to camp that day—it was much too far. Kancha was waiting for me on a little flat stretch of gravel beside some ice cliffs in the centre of the glacier. I decided to camp. We pitched our little tent and crawled inside. I was too tired to eat, and fell immediately into a deep sleep—dead to the world.

It was still dark when we started again next morning. I wanted to reach Base Camp by breakfast time, before the others had started off on any trips. We stumbled downwards. I was stiff and sore, and seemed unable to go quickly. It was eight o'clock when we forded the river and started climbing up towards Base Camp. There were some shouted greetings and I saw, with great relief, that there was a big crowd in camp. George Lowe's strong, confident figure came towards me and I felt a lifting of my burden. Everyone was there, all looking fresh and strong. I told them the whole story and then left the rescue operations in their safe and capable hands.

George Lowe and our doctor, Michael Ball, departed immediately with three lightly-laden Sherpas prepared for a fast trip up the glacier. Close on their heels went the rest of the party with food and medical supplies. I waited anxiously in Base Camp for Ball's report—rather fearing the worst. Two days later a note arrived couched in gloomy, official, medical language. But immediately on reading it some of my worry started to vanish. Ball reported that despite all McFarlane had been through, his general condition was surprisingly good. He had recovered from mild concussion; he was badly bruised in the lower part of his back with the chance of a minor fracture; he had extensive bruises on his ribs and it appeared that some of his fingers might be broken. His most serious injury was frostbite in his hands and feet, and even about this Ball was guardedly optimistic. George Lowe's message was much less restrained . . . "Jim is much better than we ever hoped—he sends his best wishes!"

It took all the Sherpas and most of the sahibs four long and hard days to carry McFarlane down over the extremely rough moraine and ice of the Barun to Base Camp. Ten miles in four days. And when he arrived he was very tired but amazingly cheerful. It was a great relief to have him safely down at Base Camp, where Ball could work on him in relative comfort. The whole party was rather done in after its rescue efforts, so we all had several days' complete rest. This was an admirable opportunity to find out all about the trips into the Iswa and the Choyang, and I cross-questioned the members of the respective parties.

When we had lost radio contact with George Lowe's party three weeks before, they'd been making slow but steady progress up the Iswa valley. The valley was U-shaped and in its lower reaches it did not receive a great deal of heat from the sun. Most of the tributary creeks were still covered with winter snow and avalanche debris, and these proved particularly difficult obstacles, as large numbers of steps had to be cut in them. The party had been fortunate on reaching the floor of the valley to find a yak track, which showed that the upper parts of the valley were used for grazing purposes by the Nepalese. But the track was hidden by a tangled mass of dead logs and bamboo sticks and obviously had not been used for some time. It was tiring work forcing a way upwards and they did not see much except fog and rain. But now and then the clouds would lift, and from the river, at 10,000 or 11,000 ft., they had seen a confusion of icy peaks rising to about 22,000 ft. These were the moments when Hardie, the surveyor of the party, would quickly assemble his photo-theodolite and take some hurried observations before the clouds closed in again.

After one particularly exhausting day, a small clearing was reached and they decided to camp. They pitched their tents and lit a fire. Then someone noticed that all around them were curious holes in the ground. Some were too small to have been made by moles and others were too large to have been made by pigs. They were quite a puzzle and there was at first some talk about digging some of them out— but nobody had the energy. Later, when the clouds cleared away for a moment, the truth was revealed. A rock precipice stretched above their heads for at least four thousand feet and falling fragments from it had caused these unusual phenomena They left rather earlier than usual next morning.

At midday on 19th April they came at last to the end of the forest and saw, only half a mile away, the terminal face of the Iswa glacier. Snow was falling and it was very cold. They sheltered under a rock, sorted out the supplies, and then sent back the six porters who were not equipped for colder temperatures. That left them a party of ten—four sahibs and six Sherpas. In very gloomy weather they pitched their camp on the glacier at an estimated height of 15,500 ft.

The next morning the sky was clear and they had their first view towards the head of the valley. Dominating the whole scene to the north was the massive four-mile-long summit ridge of Chamlang, and they could not see a single promising route in all its glassy bulges and fluted ice. West of them the glacier rose in an icefall, and above this was an array of peaks all looking exceedingly steep and difficult. To the south they were still hemmed in by the enormous rock precipices that were so characteristic of the Iswa. Only a dip in the horizon to the north-east suggested a possible line of escape to the Barun.

To establish their escape route was their first task, for this would enable them to concentrate on mapping and climbing. The Sherpas were given the job of bringing up the rest of the supplies and Lowe and Todd departed to the north-east on a reconnaissance. Meanwhile Beaven and Hardie followed up the main Iswa glacier and managed to climb with surprisingly little difficulty on to a saddle overlooking the Choyang which Evans and Harrow were exploring. Both parties returned jubilantly to camp, having been successful in finding excellent passes. Lowe reported that the exit to the Barun appeared to be relatively easy, and it was a great relief to the party to know that their line of retreat was now assured. The evening passed with a long and friendly argument as to which pass was the higher.

They now decided to move up the Iswa glacier. Next morning they found a way through a small icefall and established a new camp at over 17,000 ft. From this camp Todd and Sherpa Ang Dawa reached a high col after a long climb, of which the last few hundred feet was steep and difficult. From this col they had an excellent view into the complicated system of the Hongu valley and could see no easy route through it. At the same time Lowe and Hardie tried to reach the Hongu at a higher point farther south. Their attempt failed, for they encountered soft, dangerous snow on a steep slope at something over 20,000 ft. The following day the snow on this slope avalanched. Both of the parties had excellent opportunities for examining the complete Iswa face of Chamlang. The overhanging icecliff, the fluted ridges and the appalling steepness made perfect subjects for photography from a distance, but nowhere along the whole impressive face was there a chance for a climber to pick a reasonable route. At the end of this day all of the party were suffering from some of the effects of altitude, varying from headaches to disturbed stomachs. Despite this, the party was out climbing again next day, but once again soft and dangerous snow made them call a halt at an altitude of over 20,000 ft.

By this time the area had been fairly well covered by the photo-theodolite, and each major tributary of the upper Iswa had been examined by one of the party. On

25th April it was time to start heading towards the Barun, so they packed up and moved off down the glacier, leaving Hardie behind with a Sherpa, as he wished to finish off some theodolite work. Great was his astonishment when taking a bearing on a peak in the Choyang to see through the telescope the figures of Evans, Harrow and a Sherpa climbing it. It proved to be a fine peak of 19,600 ft.

The party met no technical difficulties on the ascent to the pass leading to the Barun, but as they were laden with the theodolite, ciné camera, tents, primuses and all the usual high-altitude equipment, they found the climb stretched their lungs and muscles to the utmost. They were not sorry to reach the crest of the pass. The descent to the more spacious Barun was quick and easy, and they enjoyed to the full the pleasures of camping again on wide grassy flats. On 27th April they walked up the valley to Base Camp, just in time to assist with the rescue of McFarlane. I felt they had done an excellent job for, as Hardie said, "We solved the problems of the Iswa headwaters, found no route on Chamlang, gave ourselves a good deal of acclimatisation, and altogether had a thoroughly enjoyable time."

The Choyang party of Evans and Harrow found the country a good deal more difficult than they had anticipated, and though they were not successful in carrying out their full plan, they did a great deal of useful work. Charles Evans gave us a very entertaining few hours when he told us the full story in his quiet dry fashion. . . .

"Geoff Harrow and I started from Sedua on 14th April. In the first two days we crossed the spur between the Kasua Khola and the Iswa and climbed to Nurgaon, a Sherpa village at 10,000 ft. on the south bank of the Iswa. Here I intended to pay off our lowland coolies and engage local men, who would know the way into the Choyang.

"We had arrived on a feast day. Everyone was out to meet us. Everyone was drunk; no one had seen anything like us before; and for half an hour we underwent an intimate inspection, and inhaled at close quarters and at second hand the fumes of chang and arak. 'Could we hire five men to carry loads into the Choyang?' I asked. Certainly. Nothing could be easier. The whole village would come with us! We could expect no more that day, and I engaged five men to start early on the morrow.

"At mid-morning they appeared, the worse for wear, and regretting their promises of the day before. It was late before we got away, and climbed to the crest through rhododendrons and magnolias, which were in full bloom, although their trunks, at 12,000 ft., were buried in deep drifts of snow.

"The track was often obscured, and the Nurgaon men found it hard going. After two days on a bleak hillside, above the treeline, in snow and mist, they said they had had enough, but that it was still many days to the head of the Choyang.

"We now had to relay our loads, and the Sherpas covered each section of the trail twice. On 18th April, after a long spell of step-cutting, we left the Iswa side of the ridge with a sigh of relief, passed through a narrow gap, and found ourselves at last in the Choyang, though thousands of feet above its floor. We were in a narrow side valley, which dived steeply into thick rhododendron bush; and the view ahead, up the Choyang, was cut off by precipitous bluffs.

"We tried for a way down into the gorge, and found ourselves in all but impenetrable bush. The red and pink blooms, which had seemed so beautiful lower down, were now reviled, and we were ready to believe what we were told later, that the middle part of the Choyang is locally considered impassable, and that the few villagers who from time to time have entered it have not yet returned.

"Unable to go down, we went up, and crossed the first bluff above its steepest part. In cloud, we made a blind descent over snow into a valley like that we had left and, unable to see farther, camped on a boulder-strewn slope. It was a day typical of our progress along the north bank of the Choyang Khola.

"Three days later, after crossing the highest of these bluffs, at 16,000 ft., we saw the head of the Choyang for the first time. It has two branches, east and west, and we were entering the east branch. At the head of the west branch were two savage-looking icepeaks, to the south of which we saw a pass leading towards the Hongu. It would be a very long way round by that route.

"However, at the head of the east branch of the Choyang, we saw a snow saddle leading straight, it seemed, for the Iswa, and east of the saddle, to the right as we looked, was a snow peak marked 19,600 ft. on our map. Ten days from Sedua, we camped, not far below the saddle. At last we had got into the upper Choyang, and our first thought, it has to be admitted, was 'How are we going to get out?' We had taken too long to get so far, and if we were to reach the Hongu at all we had to find a simple pass and cross it quickly. In the meantime we were glad to have arrived, and excited by having found, that day, as we came up to our camp, footprints that the Sherpas declared were those of the 'yeti'. They were the prints of a large animal followed by a small, and the larger prints were eight inches long by four inches broad. They were fresh tracks, probably of the previous evening, clear in hard frozen snow. At the side of the print of the sole was a rounded mark like the ball of a thumb, and at the end of the sole were the marks of toes, and of unmistakable claws.

"On 25th April I sent three Sherpas, Annullu, Changjiu and Ang Norbu, over into the Iswa to explore the pass, while Harrow and I with a Sherpa, Purchita, climbed the peak we had seen to the right of the pass. We had an exhilarating climb along high, narrow, snow ridges, and saw now the shape and origin of the Iswa glacier and the great south face of Chamlang, from which small ice avalanches were falling at intervals, but by the time we reached our peak, the usual morning cloud had come up and we could see nothing that would help us towards the Hongu. While on the summit, a thin edge of snow, we heard 'coo-ees' from the Iswa below, and were able to call to our friends, George Lowe's party, who had spotted us, though we could not see them.

"Back at camp, we learnt from Annullu that he had met George Lowe and Colin Todd on the other side of the pass, and that they had been optimistic about our finding a way to the Hongu.

"Three days later we were trying to find it. We carried our gear to the highest glacier basin of the Iswa, and climbed a very steep snow slope to a deep gash in the rock ridges which enclose the head of the valley. At noon we stood on a sharp divide of snow and rock, looking down to the Hongu, but although we could see that valley in the distance, the outlook was discouraging. The descent on the Hongu side of the pass, not difficult for unladen climbers, was too formidable for a convoy of tired and heavily-laden men, some of them inexperienced on slopes of rock and ice such as this. Moreover, the valley into which we looked ran almost south, and joined the Hongu far lower than we had expected. We had neither the time nor the necessary food to complete our planned entry into the Hongu. We must return down the Iswa, and reach the Barun Base Camp by the pass already crossed by Lowe's party.

"I started back down the slope up which we had come, with Ang Dawa, Ang Norbu and Pemba Kitar on the rope before me. The first few yards were steep, then the slope curved over into space, and our eyes met the slopes above the glacier, far below. After a few steps, Ang Norbu's foot went into a soft patch, and he heeled outwards. Ang Dawa held him, but not his load, which was attached only by a head-band; it slid out of sight and broke into fragments somewhere below; we watched it bounding and sliding down, and finally rolling to rest on the glacier.

"We resumed our cautious descent, Ang Norbu a little chagrined, but perhaps relieved to be without his burden, and no one said anything for a while, until Ang Dawa, who had been searching for an appropriate remark, came out with, 'It was just like an air drop, wasn't it?'

"That was the end of our attempt to reach the Hongu valley, and we were a very tired party when we got back that night to our camp in the Iswa.

"Two days later we had crossed into the Barun. We still had some food left, and so, instead of going up the Barun to Base Camp, we crossed the valley, and camped on the side of an attractive mountain of over 20,000 ft., which we had seen from the Iswa-Barun pass. Unknown to us, it was a mountain already climbed by Michael Ball. On 4th May Harrow and I reached the top on a most lovely morning, when Makalu, close at hand, and Lhotse and Everest, seen up the Barun valley, made a vivid and clearcut picture. By noon we were back at our high camp, and that same afternoon had found our companions at their Base Camp among the moraines of the Barun."

The accident to McFarlane and his rescue had delayed our plans, so after a few days at Base Camp we started organising our next sortie. The Californian Expedition was tackling Makalu from the south, but we had always felt that the most promising route was from the north. Certainly the slow rate of progress the Californians were making on the extremely difficult south ridge did not hold out much hope of success in that direction. We discussed the matter with the Californians and they were quite agreeable that we should investigate the northern approaches to the mountain. Our idea was to try and reach the high rocky saddle between Makalu I and its lesser neighbour to the north, Makalu II. McFarlane, Wilkins and I had an excellent look at the slopes leading to this saddle from the peak we had climbed on the way up the Barun, and we thought that the approach up the Makalu glacier looked very straight-forward, but that the last 1,500 ft. to the saddle looked rather formidable.

On 9th May the majority of the party moved up the valley and established Camp I at 17,000 ft. on the Barun glacier. My broken ribs were still troubling me a little despite the bandages, and I was forced, rather reluctantly, to stay behind. Brief notes sent down from time to time kept me well informed of the party's progress.

We had seen from our peak that the route leading up the Makalu glacier to the foot of the saddle slopes would be a tedious rather than a difficult one, and so it proved to be. The first day up the glacier was spent almost entirely in scrambling over the loose shifting moraine. Camp II was established at 19,200 ft. amongst some ice pinnacles. Next day they reached a large snowfield and established Camp II at 20,800 ft. By 12th May I had had enough of inactivity and started off with Wilkins from Base Camp to join the others. I seemed to be going reasonably well; excessive breathing gave me some pain in the chest, but I felt sure it was only temporary and would soon pass away. We had several coolies with us carrying food and equipment, but we had no tent, as we planned to spend the night at Camp II. We laboured up the long boulder-strewn slopes beside the Makalu glacier weighed down by the lethargy of altitude.

I was well ahead of the party and started searching for the site of Camp II, but I could not find it. By the time the others had caught up I was hot and very tired and not a little annoyed. The porters had to descend immediately. They had no equipment for spending the night, so we made a pile of our gear and let them go. Then Wilkins and I started searching once again for Camp II. We did not find it. It was obvious we were going to have to camp out. On a flat stretch of shingle we built some little rock walls for shelter, as the sun had gone down now and the wind was freezingly cold. We inflated our air-mattresses, put on every bit of warm clothing and then crawled into our sleeping bags. We did not have much food with us, but we shared a tin of salmon and a bar of chocolate. Lying out under the stars with the wind whistling around our noses proved, to our relief, to be far from unpleasant. With all our clothing on and inside our double sleeping bags we were really quite warm, although without the close security of a tent over our heads our little camp seemed lonely and almost rather frightening. We both slept well. In the morning everything was frozen hard and we did not move until the sun came over the shoulder of Makalu and brought a little warmth. We were just starting to pack up our camp when we heard a few cheerful voices and saw coming down towards us through the ice pinnacles half a dozen Sherpas. When they saw us they stopped in amazement.

Then they roared with laughter as we explained the reason for our night out. Camp II, they told us, was only another quarter of a mile on hidden behind the ice pinnacles.

The Sherpas had a message for us from Charles Evans. The advance party had had an interesting and successful time. They had established Camp III at 20,800 ft. on a large snow plateau. From this camp on 13th May Lowe, Hardie and Todd did a reconnaissance up on to a saddle 21,580 ft. high. It proved to be an inhospitable place in the strong, cold wind, but they could see far down on to the wild Kangshung glacier and over the barren Tibetan landscape. On the same day Evans, Harrow and Beaven concentrated on the job of finding an approach to the Makalu saddle. They made their way up on to an ice terrace which runs to the south across the face of Makalu II. At first there were some steepish pitches, but then the route improved and they found the terrace was relatively broad and easy and certainly quite safe. Finally, they had picked a camp site at a height of about 22,000 ft. and then returned down to Camp III. This had been a successful day and they decided on 14th May to follow it up. Evans, Harrow and Beaven returned with five laden Sherpas and established Camp IV on a little snowy platform under a great pinnacle of ice. On this very morning they intended pushing on up the steep slopes above.

This was excellent news. Wilkins and I felt impatient to join our companions and take an active part in the attack. We climbed up to Camp II, tucked neatly away behind the ice, and had a cup of tea and some breakfast, and then we started off up towards Camp III. It was a beautiful morning. A fresh wind was blowing but the sun was shining, and as we climbed higher the view was spreading out magnificently beneath us. We kept our eyes glued on the steep slopes high above and suddenly picked out two tiny black dots. From this distance the great snow gully they were on seemed tremendously steep and I kept hoping that the snow was in a safe condition. An avalanche there would be fatal. We were making rapid time, and although my chest was aching dully I had almost learned to ignore it. We hacked steps up the last long ice slope leading to the snow plateau and then started trudging across through the heat and the glare. The footprints seemed to go on for ever and it was a great relief when we tramped around the last snow hump and saw the tents of Camp III perched on the other side of it. George Lowe's hearty voice bellowed out in greeting and before long we were amongst our friends; our packs were taken off and hot cups of tea were thrust into our hands.

George Lowe was still bubbling with enthusiasm for the climb that he and Hardie had done the previous day. To the left of the saddle above Camp III, a very impressive snow ridge soared up to a shoulder over 22,000 ft. high. Lowe and Hardie had tackled this ridge and, after a marathon of step-cutting up its knife-edged crest, they had managed to reach the top. This had obviously been a particularly fine effort and a fair indication of their excellent state of acclimatisation.

The little dots on the snow slopes above were now very high indeed. We judged that they were at a height of over 23,000 ft., and the Makalu saddle looked tantalisingly close to them. They disappeared from view over a little crest and we did not catch sight of them again for some time. Then they were on their way down. We were very anxious indeed to hear their report and find out what conditions looked like higher up. That night in Camp III was an unpleasant one for me. I seemed to have unaccustomed difficulty in breathing at this moderate height and every cough sent a sharp pain through my chest, but I still hoped it would pass. In the morning we saw figures coming down towards us from the upper camp and we went to meet them.

Charles Evans gave us a restrained yet enthusiastic account of what they had seen. From their highest point at over 23,000 ft. the view of the difficulties ahead had been a most encouraging one. Not far away from them there appeared to be a flat stretch of snow on which a camp could readily be pitched. The snow and ice slopes above were at quite a reasonable angle, and the great steep band of rocks which were the last line of defence before the saddle had now appeared to Evans and Harrow as well broken and quite climbable. Evans was decidedly optimistic about our chances of reaching the saddle. This was very good news. I decided to push home the attack. Lowe, Hardie, Wilkins and I would go up to Camp IV on 16th May with five equipped Sherpas. From there we would establish Camp V.

It was a lovely morning on 16th May. The wind had completely dropped, and the air was still and warm. We left Camp III in excellent spirits. I led off up the steep slopes towards the ice terrace, but to my disappointment found I was completely lacking in my usual energy. I was thankful when George Lowe took over.

We reached the terrace and started the long, slow trek across it. The snow was soft and remaking the trail was a tedious business. It was none too soon for me when we climbed up the last steep slope to the little tent of Camp IV. There was very little room here, so we dug out a couple more sites in the steep slope and pitched our tents. I crawled thankfully inside.

I had a bad night, and next morning was too weak to move. Hardie had a splitting head, so Lowe and Wilkins went out and spent some valuable hours driving in pitons and fixing ropes to make the access to the snow gully safe for our Sherpas. The rest of the day was spent in the tents in mist and light snow. As we settled down to sleep there was a resounding crash, and a crevasse—four inches wide in places—opened up underneath the floors of two of our tents. It gave us a nasty shock and we took some time to calm down again. I had another bad night, and in the morning I was in a very weak condition and would obviously have to go down. In order to disturb the attack as little as possible, we decided that Hardie, who was still feeling rather poorly, should accompany me. Lowe and Wilkins started preparing for the carry to Camp V.

I commenced dressing, but seemed unable to get my boots on. George suddenly noticed my very weak condition and came to an immediate decision. All efforts must go into getting me down. A few necessities were quickly packed and then we started off. I managed to walk some of the way before everything went black. After a period of violent hallucinations and nightmare I came back to consciousness to find George tying me into a makeshift stretcher. Then followed a long period of semi-consciousness, of heat and discomfort and swinging and bumping. And then I was lying in the tent at Camp III and Charles Evans's quiet voice was telling me I was all right. Apparently I was very sick indeed. It seemed that my broken ribs had restricted the full use of my lungs and I was suffering from shortage of oxygen, extreme dehydration and perhaps malaria as well.

The party discussed what to do. It was quite obvious that it would take all their resources to get me down as quickly as possible. There seemed to be no alternative but to cast adrift our high hopes of reaching the Makalu col—disappointing as this must be. For three days the Sherpas carried my stretcher through the slippery pinnacles of ice and over the tumbled rocks and sliding moraine of the Makalu glacier. I have never seen men work harder or more willingly. But to me it seemed a very long time before we reached the Barun glacier and started across the last stretch of moraine to the comforts of Camp I.

In the thicker air of Camp I it was not long before I was well on the way to recovery. But I could not help feeling some concern at the way the time was passing. It was nearly the end of May, and as yet we hadn't really got to grips with any of our major objectives. I decided to send a strong team to tackle Baruntse—the only one of our objectives on which I now felt we had some chance of success. I had decided to travel out to Jogbani with McFarlane by the same route we used coming in, and Ball and Wilkins were to accompany us. I was very keen therefore that these two men should take advantage of the brief period before we all left to do some interesting climbing at the head of the Barun. Ball, in particular, had been giving constant care and attention to McFarlane and had therefore been tied to Base Camp. The party was divided up into two groups. Ball, Wilkins and Hardie were to go to the head of the Barun for a brief spell of climbing, and then Wilkins and Ball would return to me. Hardie then planned to make a thorough map of the area and to try to cross over the rather spectacular ridge which divided it from the Imja valley. Lowe, Beaven, Todd and Harrow were to take a strong party of Sherpas up on to the Barun plateau and lay siege to Baruntse. Charles Evans was to look after McFarlane until Ball returned, and then he would gather up the remainder of the Sherpas and equipment and join Lowe on the Barun plateau. The main body of the party would finally return to Kathmandu through the Sherpa country of Sola Khumbu.

On 28th May I had sufficiently recovered to walk down to Base Camp. I was immediately struck by all the signs of the approaching monsoon. Down the valley great tumbled clouds were rolling up; the grass was greener; there were blossoms on the scrubby rhododendrons, and myriads of tiny flowers were bursting through the arid soil. McFarlane was looking much stronger now, but he was still completely incapacitated by his frostbitten hands and feet. In the next few days we were joined at Base by Wilkins and Ball. They had taken advantage of their trip in no uncertain fashion. On 26th May they made the first ascent of Pethangtse, 22,080 ft., a peak which had often been seen and admired from the north by some of the early Everest Expeditions. On the ascent they had magnificent views of the east face of Everest appearing and disappearing in the clouds, but to their disappointment, when they reached the summit swirling mist blanketed out their view. This climb, far from tiring them, only whetted their appetite for more. To the east were two fine snow peaks of 21,500 ft. Next morning they traversed both of these peaks, hacking hundreds of steps in solid ice and overcoming some formidable problems. At this stage Wilkins had to return to Base and started down the valley with Sherpa Ang Dawa, but on the way they climbed a pleasant snow peak of 20,600 ft.

Ball had one day left and was determined to squeeze in another climb before he departed. He is an expert rock climber and his attention was inevitably attracted to a fine peak of 22,590 ft., since named Chago, on the Tibetan-Nepalese frontier immediately north of Makalu II. From the north a sweeping granite ridge with a sharp crest rose in a series of steps and ended in a thin rib of snow just before the main east–west rib of the mountain. Both Wilkins and Hardie were very doubtful of Ball's chances but, as Ball said, "New Zealanders are suspicious of rock anyhow, so I was not put off too much."

Hardie wished to do an exploratory trip over one of the passes towards Tibet, so Ball set off for Chago with Urkien. Urkien had done no rock climbing before, but was strong and active. It must have been a very fine climb indeed. Urkien kept complaining of a headache and was moving very slowly, but Ball coaxed and helped him over the difficult portions. There were three great rock steps on the ridge; Ball found a way around or up all of them and they finally reached the summit at 1 p.m. This was the highest peak the expedition had climbed at this stage and was a particularly creditable effort by Ball. He returned to us down at Base Camp and it was quite apparent to me that the four new peaks he had climbed in his brief stay at the head of the Barun had made his whole expedition well worth while.

On 30th May Ball, Wilkins and I started moving McFarlane down the valley and back to Jogbani. To carry him we enlisted the services of some of the men from Sedua who had so impressed us on the way in. We made a seat out of a packing-case, put McFarlane into it and then loaded the whole burden on to the back of one of the men. For twenty minutes he carried his load easily and confidently, and then handed over to someone fresh. We made excellent time and in my rather weakened state I had some difficulty in keeping up with the relays of carriers.

We reached the crest of the Barun pass at 14,000 ft., to find that where, two months previously, we had cut steps on steep snow slopes, now the snow had vanished to reveal a group of deep placid lakes all linked by clear rocky streams and surrounded by green turf and myriads of flowers. And then we plunged down into the heat and the monsoon; the leeches and the mud. We crossed the swaying bridge over the Arun, and forded its flooded and turbulent tributary rivers. Finally, twenty days later, extremely dirty and rather tired, we arrived at Dharan and hired a truck to travel the last thirty miles to the railhead. The rains had transformed the roads into a sea of mud, but we got through until, a mile short of Jogbani, a wheel fell off our truck. A week later we helped McFarlane aboard the plane at Calcutta and saw him fly off back to New Zealand for a long stay in hospital.[1] Wilkins, Ball and I returned to Kathmandu to await the return of the main body of the expedition and to hear their story of success or failure on Baruntse and the peaks of the Barun plateau.

[1] On his return to New Zealand from the expedition Jim McFarlane spent nearly a year in Burwood Hospital. Under the care of plastic surgeons he underwent some fifteen operations. Two fingers and part of each foot were amputated and extensive skin grafting was carried out successfully. He is now learning to walk again.

BARUNTSE—THE ICY SPIRE

GEORGE LOWE

A T Camp I on the Barun glacier I spent the night with Hillary, who was now gaining strength very rapidly after his illness high on the slopes of Makalu. We discussed the plans of the two parties: the one was to cross the mountains to the south of Everest, climbing and mapping to reach the Sherpa villages near Thyangboche monastery; the other to limp slowly down the way we had entered the mountains, carrying Jim McFarlane to the rail-head at the Indian border. It was settled that the mountain party would attempt Baruntse, map the upper reaches of the Plateau glacier, cross to the Hongu valley and from thence cross by a pass that we had used in 1952 to the Imja valley, and down to the Sherpa villages. It was agreed that 4th July was the latest date that we should meet in Kathmandu.

On 27th May four of us left the Barun valley and walked up a tributary glacier which we knew would lead us to the Plateau glacier. Nine Sherpas carried the tents and supplies that we needed for an attempt on Baruntse. On the second day we crossed the Plateau glacier and camped near the foot of Baruntse, close to a pass, the other side of which led steeply down to the Hongu valley. The ice in this part of the Plateau glacier forms gently sloping snow basins some miles in width, with an almost imperceptible tilt towards the main glacier trunk. The icepeaks that surround this unusual "plateau" jut up suddenly from the head, but the néve is astonishingly flat. As we crossed this plateau we came across an isolated block of ice, a cube some twenty feet square, resting in the middle of the glacier. New snow lay lightly all round, but despite this a scoured track of over a mile in length led across the almost flat glacier to the icecliffs near the foot of Baruntse. I cannot guess how the block could have got into this position. No other ice debris was within a mile of it, and a powerful tractor would have been needed to drag the mass—even downhill. The Sherpas talked about it for some time and decided it must have been a joke played by "abominable snowmen".

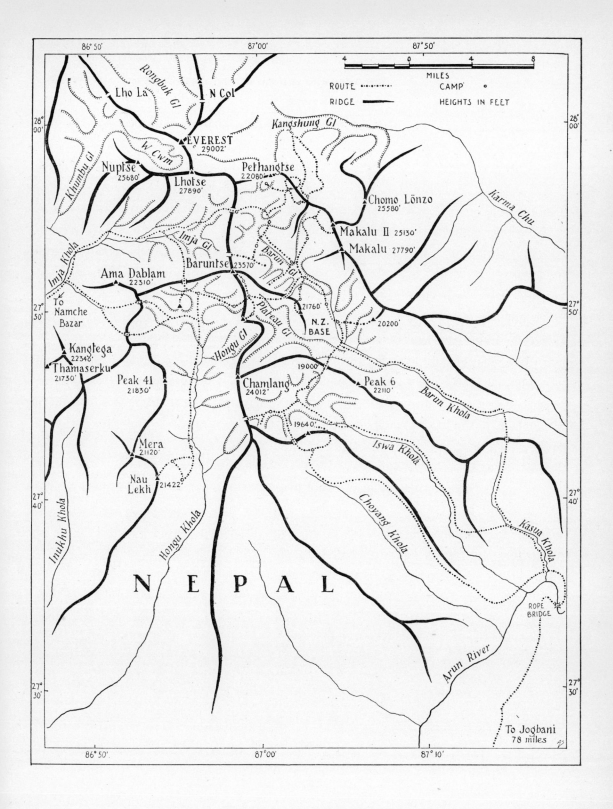

We pitched three tents on the glacier and crawled inside to rest and read, having had quite a long day traversing a pass and the head of the glacier. Not so the Sherpas. In the late afternoon they produced a rugger ball and began kicking this around on the snow. The sun set, and it was only the darkness and cold that stopped the game.

The climb of Baruntse really began from this camp. The summit was about three thousand seven hundred feet above, and we planned to put another camp on a suitable flat point on the ridge at approximately 22,000 ft. Next day this camp was placed. It was simple enough, merely a series of long snow slopes that ended in one steep pitch of about three hundred feet which required careful step-cutting. Above the camp the ridge looked broad and straightforward to a corniced point where it dipped out of sight and came into view again with broad slopes running to a rounded summit. This ridge looked deceptively easy and no one guessed that Baruntse was the belligerent, cunning, sting-in-the-tail giant that it turned out to be.

On the night of 29th May we settled down, having made all preparations for an early start next day. During the night I slept fitfully, waking continually, as it was my turn to rise at 4 a.m. to light the primuses and prepare breakfast. At first there were stars winking in the black sky, but later a wind sprang up and brought high cloud.

At half-past six we left the tents. A strong, cold wind was blowing. We were wearing suits of eiderdown under our windproofs, and our feet were encased in two pairs of woollen socks and a thick padding of kapok that composed our high-altitude boots. Over each boot was a complete canvas cover which came right up the calf of the leg, and this stopped the snow getting through the light leather of the boots. Strapped outside all this were our crampons—a set of twenty steel spikes—to give greater security on the ice slopes. The development of the high-altitude boot has now taken away the great fear of frostbite. The climb we were about to do required standing for long periods in ice-steps, and with ordinary leather boots our feet would certainly have frozen.

For the first hour we kicked steps steadily up a moderately steep snow slope. The wind threw us off balance at times but began to ease as the day grew to light. A thousand feet higher the ridge levelled off, but became much sharper and was over-hung with massive snow cornices. Bill Beaven led along the corniced ridge. The wind was blowing strongly, and we bent forward, kicking our feet rhythmically in the snow. Knowing the ridge was overhanging, we kept about thirty feet from the edge, along the steeper but safer slope.

As we moved along I called out to Beaven saying that I thought we were too close to the edge, but the wind was so strong that he could not hear over the seventy feet between us. Ahead the ridge became steeper and steeper, ending in an abrupt snow face. Beaven moved a few feet nearer to the edge of the overhang. His movements were more cautious and slow now. I was watching tensely. He kicked another step, moved his ice-axe forward and plunged it into the snow at his feet. As the axe went in there was a tearing sound. The ridge began to move. With a wild shout I leapt down the slope away from the falling edge.

Above, a long section of the snow ridge had broken away and was now thundering down the face below. Behind us, the snow that had been part of the ridge was thundering and smashing its way to the valley. I stopped in my leap thirty feet down from the breaking ridge and plunged in my ice-axe. As I twisted the rope round the axe I expected to feel the jerk of Beaven's fall. Nothing happened. My heart-beats were thumping through my clothing. As the roaring receded I looked up to see Beaven crouched on the very brink, with the yawning cliff within an inch of his boots. His ice-axe, which had caused the fracture, was still in his hand. Beaven was waving his arms gently—as a tight-rope walker does to maintain his balance.

The ridge, that had been a great curving crest, had now shorn away, leaving two hundred feet of ragged coxcomb, with my companion teetering on the very crest. Beaven stared down the abyss and quietly said, "That was bloody close". Then, without seeming to tremor, turned and moved carefully down to me, cut a large step in the ice slope and sat down in it. I joined Beaven in a similar step and then noticed a pain in my leg. In leaping off the breaking ridge, I had spiked myself with the steel crampons, tearing a hole in my clothing and my leg. I was considerably shaken and recounted to Beaven that this was my fifth experience with cornices breaking away. Beaven replied with a story of a much luckier escape from an avalanche in which he was carried down. And so we mused as I looked at the hole in my leg, which was not very serious.

By this time, Todd and Harrow had come up to us. They had not seen the incident and thought we were merely resting. Without stopping, Todd suggested that they take over the lead. It was then Todd saw that our tracks went to the very brink and stopped. He took the episode in at a glance, turned to us with a grimace and began cutting a new line of steps below the old.

For fifty feet the way was level, and then the ridge reared up steeply, making it necessary to cut steps across a steep snow face. Todd cut steadily across this. The angle became alarmingly steep. The steps were made big enough for two feet, and above the step the snow had to be sliced away to make a place for the whole leg up to the hip. The snow was in good firm condition. The wind became very gusty, and occasional cloud wreathed about us. Todd continued cutting rhythmically without rest. In just under two hours he covered about three hundred feet of steep face and turned the steepest corner. Todd shouted back that the way ahead was just as tortuous and slow—even more so, perhaps. Clouds were swirling more frequently by this time, bringing flurries of hail and snow. Beaven and I climbed across the face and, on looking round the corner, found that Todd and Harrow were only three hundred feet along cutting and clinging below the crest of the ridge. It was now an hour after midday, and the summit seemed impossibly far away. I was quite sure there would not be enough time for either pair to reach the top. With a wave we indicated our intention to the first pair and climbed down the way we had come. The descent was very difficult. Once past the place where the cornice had broken, the way was much simpler and we moved together back to the tents at 22,000 ft.

At the tent we were met by Annullu and Mingma, who had come up from the camp below with food and kerosene. We expected Todd and Harrow to return about half-past five or six o'clock at the latest, as darkness fell at this time. Light snow was falling, and as six o'clock came and went the snowfall increased; so did the wind. By half-past six it was night, and Mingma and I prepared to go out with a light. All of us were worried. We knew that if they spent the night away from the tents they would freeze to death, and if they should try to climb down the ridge where the cornice had broken they would fall off.

At seven o'clock Mingma and I set out, covered in every bit of possible clothing, carrying torches. Beaven and Annullu made ready to receive two tired climbers.

Above the tent the wind lashed us and whipped snow off the slope in such blinding drifts that we could only feel for the slope. We shouted and peered into the night. I was feeling desperately hopeless. Our shouts were whipped away by the wind. At half-past seven I was looking at my watch, fighting with a decision to give up. Mingma was bellowing into the night, when a faint answering call came from above. We flashed our lights and shouted together. The cry came again. My heart pounded; I swallowed several times and plunged uphill. Mingma saw them first, and we swept up to greet them. The wind lashed at us still. We found them sitting on the slope; both were very tired. Mingma and I joined them to our rope and we stumbled slowly back to the tents.

Baruntse had been climbed. Todd and Harrow reached the summit at half-past four. It was a grand surprise. Todd had cut steps along the ridge until half-past three, when the difficulties ended, leaving only a long, easy slope to the summit. Snow was falling and the wind was increasing. Harrow took the lead and waded steadily and relentlessly upwards for an hour to the round summit. There was no view and they began the descent immediately. The descent required the finest skills of mountaineering. Just as darkness set in they completed the descent of the broken ridge and reached easier ground. The descent had been desperate—but Baruntse had been climbed.

Two days later, Bill Beaven and I repeated the climb. We set out at six in the morning in deceptively good weather, but this switched to a most terrible day of wind and snow just as we neared the end of the very difficult piece of ridge. With the blade ridge climbed we had an hour's trudge to the summit. The wind increased, and we saw nothing but a snow-tossed whirling space. Utterly tired, with the storm becoming worse and every sign of the steps filled in and, in fact, out of sight in the swirl, we set out to climb back along the airy ridge. Fourteen rope lengths of about ninety feet each took us four and a half hours. As on the way up, Bill Beaven did all the work. He scraped out or recut the long line of steps, while I stood anchored to the slope with my ice-axe. For hour after hour I paid out the rope and watched for any sign of a slip. Had a slip occurred, I do not know what I could have done, as Beaven was a long way in front and in falling would have swung fifty or more feet like a huge pendulum and gone over a cliff. The weight would have been too great, I am sure, for the insecure axe in the very steep snow, and we should both have been plucked off.

The three pairs of gloves I wore became clogged with ice and froze into a claw shape, and when it was my turn to move I chipped hand-holds for the left hand, and hooked the frozen claw of gloves and hand into this for greater security. My hands stayed relatively warm, and worked often enough to keep them from freezing.

Several times we discussed digging a grotto into the face and sitting out the storm till next day. I am glad we did not.

Every step had to be redone. One section, the steepest, of one hundred and thirty feet took an hour and a half to descend. Darkness had now fallen, and just as the situation was becoming rather desperate we reached the last steep wall, sidled beneath the gap left by the broken cornice and moved together down the steep ridge towards camp.

Moving through the darkness we felt our way down the rest of the climb which, although quite difficult on the ascent, we now found relatively easy after the concentration needed for the ridge, now behind us.

Eight hundred feet above the tents we were met by Annullu and Mingma, who had been left at the high camp. At dark, when we did not return, they set out on their own initiative to look for us. By now a storm was raging and we were very thankful for their loyalty in coming out to meet us, despite the natural fear that Sherpas have of moving among mountains in the dark. We were as greatly relieved to see them as they were to see us. They led us back to the tents and administered to our few needs, which consisted merely of taking off our boots and helping us into our sleeping bags, where we slept for many hours.

The following day we returned to our camp on the Barun plateau. A heavy snowstorm had deposited eighteen inches of snow, and by the look of the grey billows of monsoon cloud that were daily rolling up the valleys from the plains we knew that more was to follow.

FROM WATERSHED TO WATERSHED

GEORGE LOWE

Two days after climbing Baruntse, Charles Evans arrived at the camp on the Plateau glacier with some seventeen Sherpas, who were carrying the whole of the expedition baggage across the passes to Thyangboche monastery. A bleak wind whipped snow particles across the Plateau glacier as the party trailed slowly up to our camp. Most of the Sherpas were clad in their home-made yak boots; their coats were thin, as they had been with us several months in the hot valleys. Several of the party were boys in their teens and included two girls of the same age, and it was interesting to see how matter of fact they were in accepting the biting cold and the headaches that they suffered at this altitude.

Earlier that day Beaven, Harrow, Todd and I had prospected the top of the route down the steep six hundred feet of rock that is the only practicable way off the Plateau glacier into the broad Hongu valley. Ordinarily with a small party it would be a touchy climb. It could be descended, with care needed to avoid touching off loose rocks. Now, with driving snow, iced rocks and seventeen ill-shod, not-too-able Sherpas, it was a very difficult problem. We assembled five hundred and fifty feet of heavy manilla line and fixed this over all but fifty feet of the whole descent. Most of the ropes we joined together in one long line and descended the rocks holding on to the rope, dislodging every loose or perched rock by sending them bounding and crashing down the abyss. We returned to the Plateau and assembled all the loads at the top of the slope. We then roped ourselves each to one of the ablest high-altitude Sherpas and each worked a stage of about one hundred and twenty feet up to carry down again. In this way we shepherded most of the loads and all the Sherpas down to the flat glacier in the Hongu valley. The whole operation took two very busy days. On the third we double-packed to the Hongu lake, near the foot of a pass which would take us over to the Imja valley. From there it was an easy walk down valley to Thyangboche and the Sherpa villages.

This pass did not need the four of us. Harrow was elected to lead the band and get the main baggage over the top. Evans stayed on the Plateau with the three Sherpas to complete some survey. Todd and Beaven drew the most energetic straws —straws that sent them down valley after yet one more peak—Nau Lekh, 21,422 ft. —which they climbed on 8th June, making the nineteenth peak of over 20,000 ft. climbed by the expedition. The climb was fairly straightforward and they were exceedingly fit and fast. They reached the summit along with the last clear view of the pre-monsoon time. In rain, snow and cloud they descended as the monsoon took over for the next few months. Nau Lekh was a great finish to the climbing and the exploring. It was the twenty-third ascent of the expedition and enabled a great deal of the survey to be tied together. And, of course, it also gave tempting views of still further blanks on the map that are still to be surveyed.

At the same time as we were crossing the Plateau and the Hongu-Imja divides, Hardie was performing the most exciting feat of a direct crossing across the Barun-Imja watershed by a route that had been inspected several times by Shipton and others and decided against because of its difficulty and danger. After the climb of Pethangtse and several other peaks with Ball and Wilkins, he left them to look for possible passes, and here I quote Norman Hardie's story of this exciting crossing as he wrote it for the New Zealand *Alpine Journal.*

"I now wanted to concentrate on the mapping of the Imja-Barun divide and if possible make a crossing to the Imja. I could expect two more Sherpas and some supplies two days later. A tributary glacier north of Baruntse has a col at its head. That should be examined, but as Shipton had not mentioned it, nor bothered to approach it from the Imja, there was little hope of using it for a crossing. The col farther north did sound just a little more hopeful. I had two photos of its Imja face, as well as descriptions by Shipton, Hillary and Evans, and there, too, the chances of finding a safe route were not very likely. I decided to inspect the first col with Urkien, and when the two reinforcements arrived examine the one which presented the better possibilities.

"On the day after Ball left, Urkien and I carried our camp to the glacier north of Baruntse. In the afternoon I had ideas about a 20,750-ft. subsidiary of that peak. Urkien asked what its name was.

" 'It has no name.'

" 'What can you see from the top?'

" 'If we see anything it will be about the same as from the second peak I climbed with Pasang Dawa.'

" 'If it had a name I could see why you would want to climb it.'

" 'Why not climb mountains and then give them names?'

"He thought that was a wonderful idea, but his suggestions were not so good. First he thought of all the names of the expedition members. I dismissed these. Then he recited the names of his three young sisters. It was time to start up the mountain. We did climb it. On the summit, clouds obscured all but my very capable and strong companion, wearing a frozen coating of snow on his pigtail. Later I met his young sisters and I thought Urkien's idea was not so bad after all.

"Early on the 31st we set out for the col overlooking the Imja. The climb up the glacier was relatively easy, but far above, on our left, were some menacing bulges of ice on Baruntse. The last three hundred feet to the col were of steep rock. I decided to let Urkien lead up this, making him the first to tread any part of the Imja-Barun divide, and he would see the headwaters of his own district. When we faced the rock, I realised that this idea was hopelessly unwise. Here the rock was abominably loose and steep, and I decided to go first. Slowly I gardened and sidled all the way up, eventually reaching the col, gasping for breath, and grasping for something solid. Urkien followed on a tight rope and perched behind me, astride the ridge. Below, in the Imja, a horrid face of steep ice flutings disappeared into the clouds 2,000 ft. beneath our left feet. Urkien was bitterly disappointed. He was in a hurry to reach the Sola Khumu. Through a clearing in the clouds we did get a glimpse of Chukhung, the top village in the Imja, but before long snow was falling. We returned, picked up our camp in the afternoon, and on the way back to the 19,000-ft. camp met the reinforcements, Ang Dawa and Aila.

"We took stock of our position. Our food supplies would last for two weeks. Besides the usual high-altitude equipment, there were twenty-five pounds of survey gear. We would be too heavily laden to attempt the Imja crossing immediately, but I had told Evans that if I had not completed the crossing within seven days, I would make my exit via the Plateau, where I would meet him in the Hongu valley. Early on 1st June we set out for the more hopeful of the two Imja cols, intending to climb some peaks from it and then examine the other side. We crossed the Barun glacier and climbed up the tributary descending from the col. In a snowstorm, camp was pitched at about three hundred feet below the col.

"Urkien and Ang Dawa were sent back next day to bring up the remainder of the 19,000-ft. camp, and in the meantime Aila and I, without much visibility, ascended the last face to the divide and looked down. Each low point was inspected, but at only one was there any sort of hope. I cut steps down it for the full extent of the one hundred feet of rope. Aila nervously followed, and when he reached me he said that laden Sherpas could never get down this slope. We waited for a while. Some of the clouds lifted, and Ama Dablam stood up with its awful steepness. The Imja pass to the Hongu was easily located, but the tremendous face of Lhotse, now in profile just two miles away, was the fairy-tale mountain, impossible and frightening. There just might be a route on the second peak of Lhotse from where I was standing, but it would be very long and difficult.

"Below me was the Imja, but after the initial steep pitch and then an easier portion I could not see the last five hundred feet. Back at camp Aila saw I had six pitons, so he forgot the steepness and declared there was a route down. When the others returned they heard his news, and there were wonderful tales of chang and potatoes in the Sola Khumu. I was not so sure. One needs a lot of rope, small loads and a fast party for a piton descent on a long complicated slope.

"On 3rd June Ang Dawa and Aila packed most of our gear to the col. Urkien and I climbed the large domed ice peak, 22,060 ft., to the south. The people in the Imja refer to this mountain as Cho Polu. Yet at a later date when I asked the lama of Dingboche which was Cho Polu he seemed very vague, and pointed in a broad sweep to the head of the valley. The ridge had a variety of ice, snow, rock and cornice, and the climb of a little more than two thousand feet took about four hours. By the time we were on the summit, clouds had obscured what should be a very good view. There seemed to be more soft snow about than at any time in the last two weeks. Was the monsoon coming? . . . In the afternoon I cut down to the bottom of the first steep portion below the col, some three hundred feet, but the whole route was not yet solved.

"Urkien has better judgement than Aila. It was obvious to Urkien that the crossing could never be easy. There was distinct change of mood in the tent. I was put under great pressure to cross to the Kangshung, Rongbuk, and return to Nepal via the Nangpa La. I resisted the strong temptation. Aila woke me during the night to listen to the wailings of a yeti. Unfortunately the cries ceased as I became conscious.

"By 9 a.m. all our loads were on the col. I hammered in two pitons, joined together two ropes of one hundred feet, and on to them I tied fifty feet of nylon tent cords. I renewed the steps to the limit of the rope, brought the Sherpas down, lowered the loads to the platform below and withdrew the pitons, still having six in the bag. I could climb that one again if necessary. The rest of the ice below consisted of a steep face having a series of enormous bulges, separated by crevasses, but showing few signs of collapse. Between the bulges were three channels disappearing down into the clouds. Ang Dawa and Aila went to examine the nearest channel, while Urkien and I had a look at the other two. This operation took some time, and many steps were cut. It was midday by the time we were together again and a decision made. We would take the nearest route. Admittedly some soft snow had probably gone down it in the last week, but we would not be in it for long, and there seemed to be many ways of jumping out of it in a hurry if necessary. The lads loaded up to more than sixty pounds each.

"The theodolite, now a white elephant, remained on the snow. I put it on top of my thirty pounds, and uttered something strong. The other three were on one hundred feet of rope. I was tied on the end of the other hundred. When a long series of steps were required I would use a karabiner and slip on to the first man. On two occasions icy pitches gave so much trouble that I had to climb up past the others to support them on their descent. Once again the pitons were invaluable. I could hammer my pack to the ice before climbing up, and then they made the belays certain. Aila was delaying progress so much, and, poor fellow, collecting so much from my tongue, that he dumped fifteen pounds of tsampa. He was much better after that. As I came past the forlorn heap I thought what a strange place for the ending of a kitbag branded 'New Zealand Alpine Club Himalayan Expedition'. When we were over half-way to the Imja, we suddenly met an enormous crevasse which could not be outflanked. Below it we could see a reasonable route all the way to the bottom. We lowered everything to its lower lip, leaving a piton in the upper. The rate of progress increased. I led down a steepening couloir, and again ran into hard ice. I had just completed the steps when Ang Dawa, above, slipped. Aila held him. It was not his first major slip in the past week. Urkien at the rear called out, 'Sahib, we pass'. This was a request that I resume the rear position. Half an hour later our worries were over. We camped at 6.30 p.m. far out on the Imja glacier. I took pity on my companions for the loss of their tsampa, and for the abuse I had hurled at them.

I gave away most of the reserve food. It was not for another day that Urkien confessed that he had five extra pounds of tsampa in his pack.

"On the 5th we were right out to Chukhung, among flowers, yaks and real grass again. Here we bought a leg of yak, some potatoes and a quart of arak. How long was it since we had a real day of rest? On the 7th Urkien was sent home to Khumjung with the survey and other surplus gear, while we three returned up the Imja valley and met Harrow and the main Sherpa team coming out of the Hongu. Later in the day I crossed to the Hongu, having Annullu as an escort to the top of the pass. I located Evans's camp and spent the night in his tent. On the 8th I again caught the main party and prepared for the social activities at Khumjung, the luxury of Ang Tsering's cooking and a sleep on grass."

The monsoon arrived early in 1954. Usually it takes command of the weather about the second week in June. From its arrival until some time in September the monsoon brings rain, snow and cloud during the warm growing season of what might be called summer. During the monsoon climbing expeditions usually leave the Himalaya. Before we did so we wished to experience the Sherpa ceremony of Dumji.

For the past month the Sherpas had been telling us of the ceremony of Dumji. They were continually counting on their fingers how many days were left before Dumji. At Dumji there were dancing, feasting and frolics lasting for five days. I decided, after climbing Baruntse, that Dumji was the thing I most wanted to see. If there were any doubts in my mind between wanting to climb and wanting to see the Sherpa ceremony, it was swept aside on discovering that every year one family is required to supply the food and drink for ceremonies. It so happened two of our Sherpas, Mingma Tsering and Ongi Gyalbo, were the men responsible to the village of Khumjung. I promised to get them to Khumjung before Dumji began on 10th June. The quickest possible way was to cross the Mingbo La. This pass had not been crossed before, but had been reached from the other side by Charles Evans during the training climbs before the ascent of Everest.

By the beginning of June the monsoon was making itself felt. The daily snowstorm got longer. The low cloud rolled up the valleys earlier and stayed later. The temperature grew ominously warmer. The snow became wet and dangerous. Mingma Tsering, Ongi Gyalbo and I left the main party at the Hongu lake on 6th June. About a mile down the valley we struck up a tributary glacier that led to the Mingbo La. All the glaciers in the Hongu valley are a wilderness of debris, chiefly rock being ground off the mountain walls. This glacier had a huge lake in the terminal ice which took some hours to get round. Higher, the clear ice of the glacier was melting, although covered with new, wet snow. Walking on it made it settle with a dull thump—an ominous condition that caused me heartaches for the next two days. The snow conditions were very dangerous.

We camped four hundred feet below the pass. The altitude was about 19,000 ft., and all night a curious mixture of rain and snow fell, easing slightly at dawn as we set out for the crossing. From the start we wallowed in wet, thigh-deep snow. After three hours we reached the pass. The clouds had lifted a few hundred feet, and from the pass I looked across the Hongu valley to Baruntse. The summit was in cloud. Ama Dablam emerged for a few minutes only and then the clouds wrapped round this beautiful mountain.

The Thyangboche side of the pass was very steep for the first three hundred feet, and then it was flat across a glacier plateau. This plateau was covered for about fifty acres with ice avalanche debris from cliffs over a mile away. After step-cutting we reached the flat covered with debris. New snow had covered most of the jagged ice blocks and instead of walking across we plunged through up to our thighs. Walking and falling became so frustrating that we took off our packs, and by crawling and various crab-wise actions we dragged our packs and made faster progress than by persisting in an upright position.

During these antics the cloud came down and we found our way out of the avalanche area on to firm ice where we could walk upright again. Getting off the ice caused us some worry, as the mist made us grope among crevasses and ice walls in wet, soggy, oozy snow and silent, dripping icicles. In the early afternoon we climbed down the lower end of the glacier, found a stony ablation valley in the mist and began hurrying. From the pass we descended about six thousand feet and my legs nearly gave out.

Late in the evening, we reached trees, and with Mingma and Ongi singing and shouting at the joy of homecoming, we reached a yak herding-place called Yaren. Yaren was only an hour's walk from the Thyangboche monastery and it was our first view of grass, trees and flowers for over two months. Here we had the first fresh potatoes, yak curds and milk that we had had for about the same time. In the yak-herder's hut, the smell of yaks was strong, but I slept like a log, in deep hay. On

8th June we reached Kundi village after calling in at Thyangboche monastery, where we drank tea with the lamas and arranged a day after Dumji for the presentation of Coronation medals to the Sherpas who carried above Camp VII on Everest.

By the 12th June all six of us were gathered together near the village of Khumjung, where we attended the various ceremonies of Dumji, having some of the most memorable days of the expedition with the hospitable Sherpas.

DUMJI—A FIVE-DAY FESTIVAL

GEORGE LOWE

THE annual ceremony of Dumji is looked forward to eagerly by everyone in the Khumbu villages. Dumji is in many ways similar to a harvest festival. It is strongly religious, being centred on the village gompa or church, with the lamas running almost constant prayers for the five days. Each year the lamas of Thyangboche move down to the surrounding villages to officiate.

During Dumji I stayed in Mingma's house, and there I was at the very hub of the ceremony. Every year one family is required to supply the food and drink for the whole village for the gompa festivities. This year it was Mingma's turn. On the first day the lamas came to his house and blessed the food. They sat down to take tea, which was served Tibetan style, and during this, several gallons of old yak butter were produced and moulded on boards into various shapes and rhythmic patterns of stars, crescents, moons and fans.

These patterns were then painted with water colours in bright strips of orange, black, red, yellow and green. A great deal of discussion went into the preparation and final presentation of the decorations.

In the evening the altar in the gompa was decorated with the butter decorations. Every family supplied a small brass chalice, complete with oil and a wick, and each lamp was lit and kept burning during the five days. When the decorations were complete, the altar was a beautiful sight with colourful butter symbols, lit by sixty clear burning lights. In the middle of this were the crowns of three human skulls, and these, I thought, were a macabre, unusual touch that did not seem to fit the mood.

All these decorations and others were placed in the gompa the afternoon before the five-day ceremony began. Sitting in the gompa—and missing all the fun of the modelling—was the oldest lama of all. He looked very pious and divorced from the mundane things of the world, but looks are not everything. A stray dog wandered into the gompa and began sniffing the butter decorations. The smell interested him greatly, and he moved closer for a longer and better smell. This was rudely interrupted when he was landed a terrific wallop in the ribs from a stone hurled by the old lama. I looked up to see him rocking imperceptibly and chanting prayers with the slightest grin of satisfaction on his withered face. It seems the lama keeps a bag of stones handy for precisely this purpose, and takes delight in his pastime as guardian.

In Mingma's house a potato feast began, followed by a *chang*-tasting session. That evening four wooden barrels of *chang* were unsealed, five months after brewing. The *chang* for Dumji is brewed in the autumn and set down in wooden barrels and sealed over the top with a suitable consistency of yak dung. *Chang* is a beer brewed from different grains, and the brews vary considerably. There is rice *chang*, millet *chang*, maize *chang* and unidentified *chang*. *Rakshi* is made by distilling the *changs*, and is usually a clear spirit of fiery potency.

When the barrels were opened, a tasting committee formed and discussed the merits of the different barrels by sniffing, holding to the light and weighing the merits of the vintage like professional tasters. The brews vary in colour; the best, I thought, was rice *chang*. From the rice barrels flowed an amber clear fluid of mild taste and little alcoholic potency. Rice *chang* is a very good drink. Below the amber was a messy sludge which is rather like alcoholic porridge, and this, too, is drunk.

There are no beds in a Sherpa house. They sleep on mats on the board floor covered by a yak-hair rug. I slept in my sleeping bag and was constantly waging a poison war on the fleas and bugs that infest the houses. For me the day began at 5.30 with a mug of clear *chang*, while the potatoes were steaming. Potatoes are never boiled properly, as the boiling-point of water is well below 212° F. at this village, 14,000 ft. above sea-level. By 5.30 the girls of the house were up sweeping and cleaning, having already made the twenty-minute journey to the nearest stream to fetch water. At the stream the women used to gather for gossip before five o'clock in the morning.

Nearly every morning the monsoon brought rain, and I lay inside reading. During the afternoons I went visiting. Visiting in Sherpa-land is very like home, except that you do not knock—just step through the door on the ground floor, past the young yaks, firewood and leaves, climb thirteen steep, dark stairs to a very black corner and then turn hard left and grope along the wall to light and the large main living-room. Turn hard left, for if you do not, another step takes you into the Sherpa lavatory, a room with a thick layer of leaves on the floor and the floor has a hole in the centre.

Once inside, you sit cross-legged on carpets near the window and accept a glass of *chang*, which is three times offered to you, thrice filled as you drink; then the formality is over and you may sit and talk. Tea is then prepared by boiling compressed tea-leaves, adding salt and yak butter while the hot liquid is churned in a long thin churn. The churned brew is then reheated and put in great brass kettles and served steaming hot. The tea-cups are Chinese, and some of them are of fine bone china, without handles, set in silver stands with decorated lids which are popped on the cup to keep the tea warm. Although it is called tea, the taste resembles nothing like our conception of tea and is more like a greasy soup. I found it very thirst-quenching and a mild laxative.

For Dumji everyone produced their finest clothes. All the women had colourful sashes and gleaming hair decorations. Everybody—men, women and children—combed their hair with wooden combs, rubbed in oil or butter and plaited the gleaming black tresses into long pigtails, and surmounted this with embroidered and fur-trimmed hats.

All day at the gompa prayers were being intoned, accompanied by cymbals, drums and horns. Early in the afternoon there were very few people about except some men erecting an awning over the open square immediately in front of the main building. The material was a collection of various expedition tent-cloths joined in odd patterns. But most interesting to me were the ladders that they were using, which were none other than the complete sections of a duralumin ladder that we had left in the Khumba icefall during the Everest expedition the previous year. They told me they had ascended the icefall after the expedition and dug the various ladders out of the ice where we had left them.

In the evening, several dances were performed by four of the lamas, during which rice grains were flung about. It was a slow, stately, turning dance, placating the gods for good crops and a fair season. The first days of Dumji were comparatively quiet, and it was during the last two days that the intensity grew to continual excitement with noisy dancing, and a constant rumble of prayers with drum rolls and cymbals to punctuate the climaxes.

On the third day there were dances which degenerated into a crude mime of the "abominable snowman" chasing the girls of the village. For this, the hairy scalp which the Sherpas claim is the scalp of the "yeti" or snowman was worn on the dancer's head, and his dress was made of sheepskins. Another dance, which left everybody in paroxysms of mirth, was a ribald dance of an old man who danced sadly about feeling the frailty and sadness of age, and then, when a young girl danced in (this part was played by a man who had been with our expedition), the frail grandpa leaps for joy and gives chase, having forgotten his age.

The most elegant and dramatic act of Dumji occurred on the last evening. In the square in front of the gompa a fire was started under a great cauldron of yak butter. Ten feet above the cauldron were a series of calico strips inscribed with prayers hanging from bamboo poles. A young lama dressed in fine silks and wearing a new pair of white and red felt boots with deep cushion soles and pointed toes began incantations as the butter began to boil. He spun and stepped in circles round the fire, with a bowl of *rakshi* held high above his head. An orchestra of horns and drums accompanied all this. The tempo of the music increased as did the dance, and with a clash of cymbals the dance reached a showy climax when the lama poured the bowl of pure spirit into the boiling butter. There was a flash of flame like petrol igniting. The prayer flags were devoured and sparks and prayers flew heavenwards.

Their folk dances are unusual in that they are performed by linking arms abreast and begin with a long, wailing chant and with very slow, rocking foot rhythms. These gradually increase in tempo with the music, and finish with everyone hissing the rhythm and whirling and stamping their feet with the fire of a Cossack dance.

The origin of Dumji is obscure. The Sherpas say they have always celebrated this festival, and yet claim that it did not come with them from Tibet. Their migration from Tibet has occurred in the last few hundred years. Their houses, clothes, food and language are all strongly Tibetan, but they are proud of their Nepalese nationality and look down on Tibetans as slightly inferior. Although the customs are strongly Tibetan, they apply Nepalese law to buying and selling land, to marriage and divorce, and to justice for criminals. In the last few years a band of robbers have flourished in the wild passes above the Sherpa villages. Robbery with violence and murder had increased so much that the people banded together under a young lama who organised a party to chase the culprits if they robbed again. Being Buddhist, they agreed not to kill the robbers but to bring them to a village trial. A robbery was then committed and five culprits were caught after a chase. One was shot in the leg after a beating, all admitted the robbery and gave evidence against the others. The robbers were all murderers, and a village meeting was held where a decision was made as to whether Tibetan or Nepalese punishment should be meted out. The first was immediate and drastic—either the breaking of both knees and stiffening their joints, or the cutting off of both hands, either of which made robbery with murder too difficult to continue. The robbers sighed with relief when the lama made the decision to march them under escort to the head village of the Nepalese district, where they would stand trial and perhaps undergo imprisonment, according to the law of Nepal.

Sherpas marry at ages between eighteen and twenty-four, and usually to partners of their own choice. Not all marry, and there are several bachelors and spinsters of all ages in the villages. Marriages are not solemnised by the church. It is a family affair, marked by a day of feasting attended by family and friends. Marriages can be dissolved by mutual agreement and payment of a moderate sum of money to the wife, but divorce is not very common.

After the ceremonies of Dumji, we were entertained at a gala dinner at Da Tensing's house, where our sixteen expedition Sherpas acted as hosts. There was a great feast followed by Sherpa dances which continued until near dawn.

Next day we all walked to Thyangboche monastery with the lamas and the Everest Sherpas (or their fathers or wives if the man was not available), and there we presented twelve Coronation medals to the Sherpas who had carried loads there in 1953. These medals were awarded by Her Majesty the Queen and had been sent to us by Sir Christopher Summerhayes, the British Ambassador in Nepal. Charles Evans, who was the deputy leader of the Everest expedition, performed the impressive ceremony.

Charles Evans also presented the Cullum medal of the American Geographical Society, which was awarded to the team of Sherpas for their part in the climbing of Everest. The medal was of real gold, and was considerably larger than a crown piece and worth a great deal of money. It was decided to leave the medal on show in the custody of the lamas of Thyangboche on behalf of all the Sherpas. A document was made out in English, Tibetan and Nepali explaining the ownership of the gold medal, and this is held by the Sherpa headman in case arguments should arise over ownership.

The medal ceremony was an impressive occasion, and after the lama's invitation we stayed the night in the monastery. We ate their food, which consisted of rice, potatoes, curds and bowls of Tibetan tea. We slept on a covered terrace outside the monastery, and it rained heavily during the night and the roof leaked. Next day we gave a gift of two hundred rupees, but did not mention the roof. We had a breakfast of potatoes, chupatties and tea, after which we were presented with ceremonial scarves as tokens for a safe journey. With this blessing, and with such a flood of hospitality, it was hard to leave the land of the Sherpas.

On 20th June, with the monsoon rains firmly in control of the weather for two months, we reluctantly packed our camp and began the long walk of some one hundred and seventy miles to Kathmandu.

EAST OF EVEREST

A dragon outside the temple in Dharan, symbolically guarding the entrance to Nepal.

The expedition caused great interest at Jogbani, which is the end of the rail journey through India.

Small boats on the Ganges river.

At Jogbani these buffalo unloaded jute and later hauled our four tons of baggage to waiting motor trucks.

The choosing of a good ice-axe is very important, and first choice was given to Da Tensing, the sirdar, and Dawa Thondup, his chief lieutenant.

PREPARATIONS IN DHARAN BEFORE
THE MARCH TO THE MOUNTAINS.

Da Tensing and Charles Evans decide the quantities of local grain.

Edmund Hillary

Charles Evans

George Lowe

Norman Hardie

Geoff Harrow

Jim McFarlane

Bill Beaven with Ang Temba

Colin Todd

Brian Wilkins

Da Tensing

Michael Ball

The journey to Base Camp, which took fifteen days, began over pleasant hill paths from Dharan.

Evans, Lowe and Hillary, three experienced Himalayan travellers, used umbrellas to shield the sun and deflect the monsoon rain.

Nepali porters on the march to Khanbari.

Khanbari was the last bazaar of any size, and here we bought supplies of rice and flour. New porters were engaged, and these were local farmers used to the rigorous travel in the higher mountain valleys.

For some days we followed a trade route along the banks of the Arun river, where camps were made near shelter rocks in thick jungle. The hill porters cooked their meals of grain over smoky fires and slept under rocks.

Crossing the swift Kasua river on the route from the Arun to the Barun.

Late winter snow lay at 12,000 ft., below the pass that leads to the Barun valley. Many of the porters carried over this in meagre clothing and flimsy footwear.

Lowe and Beaven sleeping during the breakfast halt.

McFarlane, Ball and Hillary taking a round of angles on the peaks.

Ang Norbu and Mingma brewing porridge over a smoky juniper wood fire.

Harrow crossing the icy Barun river below the glacier snout.

Base Camp in the Barun was about 16,000 ft. at the foot of Makalu. Camping on grass among hardy shrubs from which we made wood fires made this a pleasant base, close to the peaks to be explored.

This view of Makalu was seen by Lowe's exploratory party which mapped the Iswa river mountains. After the survey, the party crossed a pass of 19,000 ft. to the Barun valley.

Peak 6, an unnamed peak of 22,000 ft., that divides the Iswa and Barun valleys. No easy route to the summit present

elf from any side of the mountain. The snow saddle on the right proved to be a good way out of the Iswa valley.

The gorges of the lower Iswa were heavily forested, and six days were needed to make six miles to the glacier. From the bush, tantalising glimpses of Peak 6 urged us forward. (*Inset*) Hardie surveying with photo-theodolite.

While mapping the Barun glacier, Hillary, McFarlane and Wilkins placed this camp near Lhotse (27,890 ft.). McFarlane and Wilkins, while returning from a survey, plunged through a snow-covered hole in the ice and fell sixty feet. McFarlane was seriously injured. Wilkins extricated himself and went for help.

McFarlane spent a night in the crevasse which caused severe frostbite of his hands and feet. Next day he was pulled to the surface and carried to camp. Five days later, after an exhausting stretcher journey from 19,000 ft., he was resting safely at Base Camp.

In Base Camp at the foot of Makalu we rested and decided to reconnoitre the approaches to this mountain from the north.

Four camps were placed on Makalu and the route went easily up to 23,000 ft.
Camp II (19,000 ft.) alongside the Makalu glacier.

At Camp IV (22,000 ft.) Hillary, who earlier had broken some ribs in the crevasse accident, collapsed and became delirious. Hillary was carried to Camp I, where he quickly recovered.

McFarlane's frostbite crippled his hands and feet and he was transported in a carrier made from a provision box. Eight strong men from Sedua village took turns to carry McFarlane 150 miles in twelve days.

McFarlane was carried across the Arun river bridge by a huge man called 'Muscles'. This was a nerve-racking crossing, as the bridge swayed with the wind, and everything depended on the man's skill in carrying his load across a thin footway of twisted vines.

Many peaks were climbed, and here Chomo Lonzo (25,580 ft.) is seen from a peak to the north-west (21,530 ft.), climbed by Ball, Wilkins and Hardie.

28

Makalu (27,790 ft.) from the summit of Pethangtse, climbed by Ball, Hardie, Wilkins and Sherpa Urkien.

Hardie's camp in the Imja valley after his difficult crossing of the Barun divide. Ama Dablam is the peak in the distance.

Baruntse (23,570 ft.), as seen from the Imja glacier, shows only steep cliffs which hide the true summit.

Baruntse was climbed by a very difficult ice ridge by Todd, Harrow, Beaven and Lowe.
This picture shows Todd cutting steps across the first of many steep exposed snow faces.

Todd negotiating a steep ice corner on the ridge of Baruntse.

Chamlang (24,012 ft.) from the Hongu valley.

Todd photographing monsoon clouds approaching Na

kh (21,422 ft.), the last peak climbed by the expedition.

The Kangshung face of Everest from a high camp at the head of the Barun glacier. The long north-east ridge shows in its entirety, with the South Summit and south-east ridge to the left.

Early in June six members of the expedition crossed the mountains to the Sherpa village of Khumjung. The approach to a Sherpa village is marked by the building of a chorten—a circular stone monument as shown above.

Sherpas are devout Buddhists and much of their community life is centred around the gompa or local place of worship. Here families of Khumjung village have assembled to celebrate the feast of Dumji—a sort of harvest festival. Rice cakes and millet beer are supplied by certain families and is given to all during the prayers and chanting.

People who reach old age are cared for by their families and spend much of their time spinning silver prayer wheels which contain tightly wrapped scrolls of up to fourteen thousand prayers. This old man chanted *"Om mane padme hum"* (Hail the jewel in the lotus flower) as he turned his prayer wheel.

Statues of Buddha are found in all the gompas, but few are as jewelled or as sacred as the figure in Thyangboche monastery. Surrounding the statue are many shelves which contain manuscript books of prayers carefully wrapped against dampness and damage.

The prayer *Om mane padme hum* is repeated in many forms. Above is a wall of newly carved stones repeating the prayer on each block.

Some of the fifty bronze prayer drums that are set into the wall around the monastery of Thyangboche. All repeat the same prayer.

Mingma Tsering and his wife have two young children, the youngest was born while Mingma was with the expedition. Mingma was a well-to-do man of twenty-five and his wife was twenty-two. They had been married three years.

Visitors are always invited to drink a local beer, called *chang*, while salted tea is being prepared. Visiting in the afternoon is an established custom and drinking ritual is always observed.

George Lowe in Sherpa dress. Lowe, who was Mingma's guest for some weeks, persuaded his host to take this—his first photograph.

At Thyangboche monastery Charles Evans, deputy leader of the expedition, handed to the Abbot the American Geographical Society's Gold Medal. The award was made to the Sherpas who carried high on the successful Everest expedition, and was left with the Abbot of the monastery for safe keeping.

Charles Evans presents the Coronation medal to Da Tensing at the ceremony in Thyangboche monastery. These medals were awarded by Her Majesty the Queen to the Sherpas who carried to the South Col of Everest during the successful expedition of 1953.

Not all the men awarded Coronation medals were able to attend the Thyangboche ceremony. Pasang Phutar was away with another expedition; his eldest child was brought and received the medal. This pleased everybody.

After the presentation of Coronation medals each member of the expedition received a white scarf from the Abbot of the Monastery. The scarf carried with it the prayers for a safe journey. *Front row:* Charles Evans, George Lowe, Colin Todd and Da Tensing. *Centre:* Norman Hardie, Bill Beaven and Geoff Harrow. *Back row:* Urkien, Kuncha, Ang Dawa and Ang Temba.

Late in June, as the wet monsoon covered the mountains with new snow we regretfully left the land of the Sherpas at this chorten near the foot of Kantega and began the long march to Kathmandu.